Illustrations

of

a

Generation

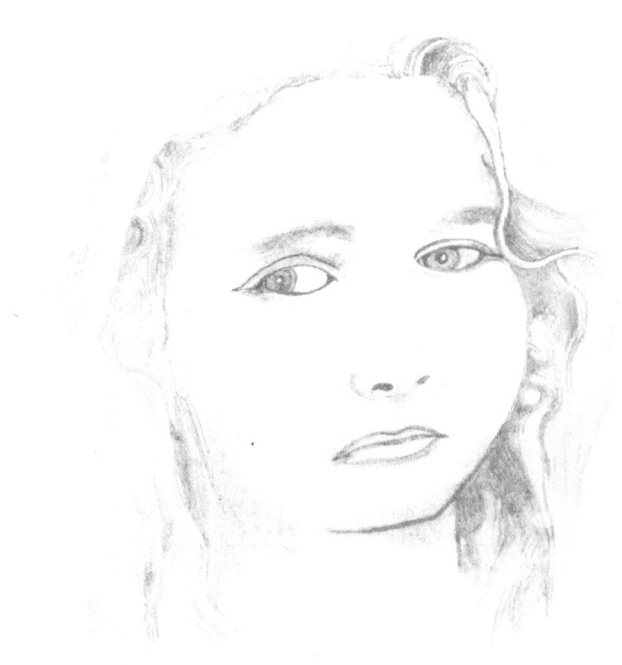

"Illustrations & Paintings
by Louise Harrison"

Compiled & Edited by Philip R. Harrison

Illustrations & Paintings by Louise Harrison
Copyright c Louise Harrison 2014

Paintings by Mary Harrison
Copyright c Mary Harrison Estate 2014

First Edition

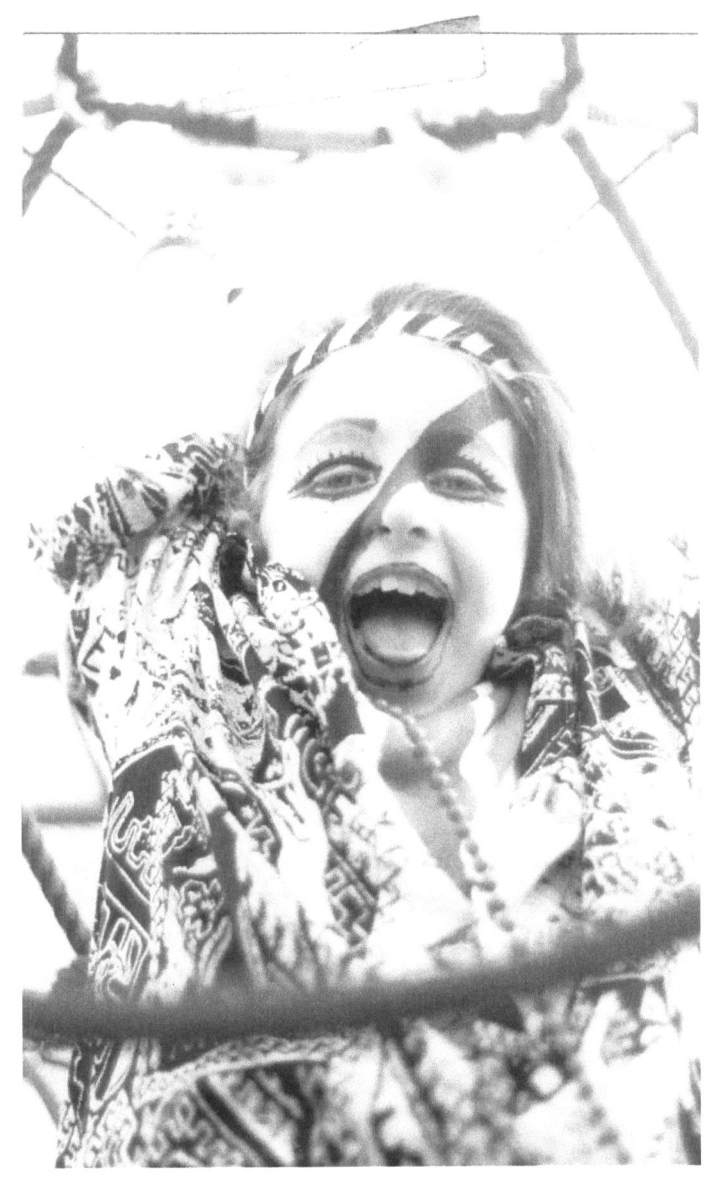

LOUISE - AGED 10

(Louise Harrison is now 31 and lives in Middlesex, England)

Contents

Mary Harrison

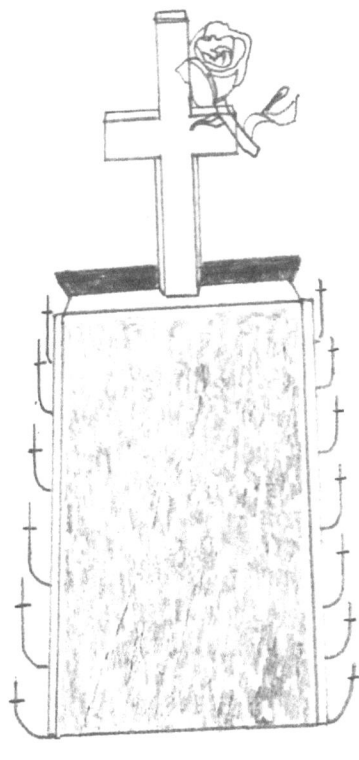

Forward

The illustrations and paintings in this book are the astonishing works of my Sister and Mother.

The first twelve illustrations were created to be part of my first novel, There's More To Life. These illustrations mysteriously disappeared during the production of the book and thus the book went on sale on Amazon without these invaluable drawings within it's pages.

Some time later, whilst clearing my garage out I happened upon these lost memories with great delight. With the support from their creator, my Sister and I agreed to compile the pictures in to this current book for all to enjoy in the craft and skill of the artist.

Louise added to this precious collection with her present day style of illustrations to demonstrate her variety and depth as an artist.

Along with these masterfull works of art we both feel honoured to showcase our Mother's beautiful paintings donated to this book by our father, Laurence Harrison.

Illustrations of a Generation from Mother to Daughter.

Enjoy!

Philip R Harrison

There's More To Life

www.theresmoretolife.webs.com

The Adventures Of Fluffy Monkey Series

www.theadventuresoffluffymonkey.webs.com

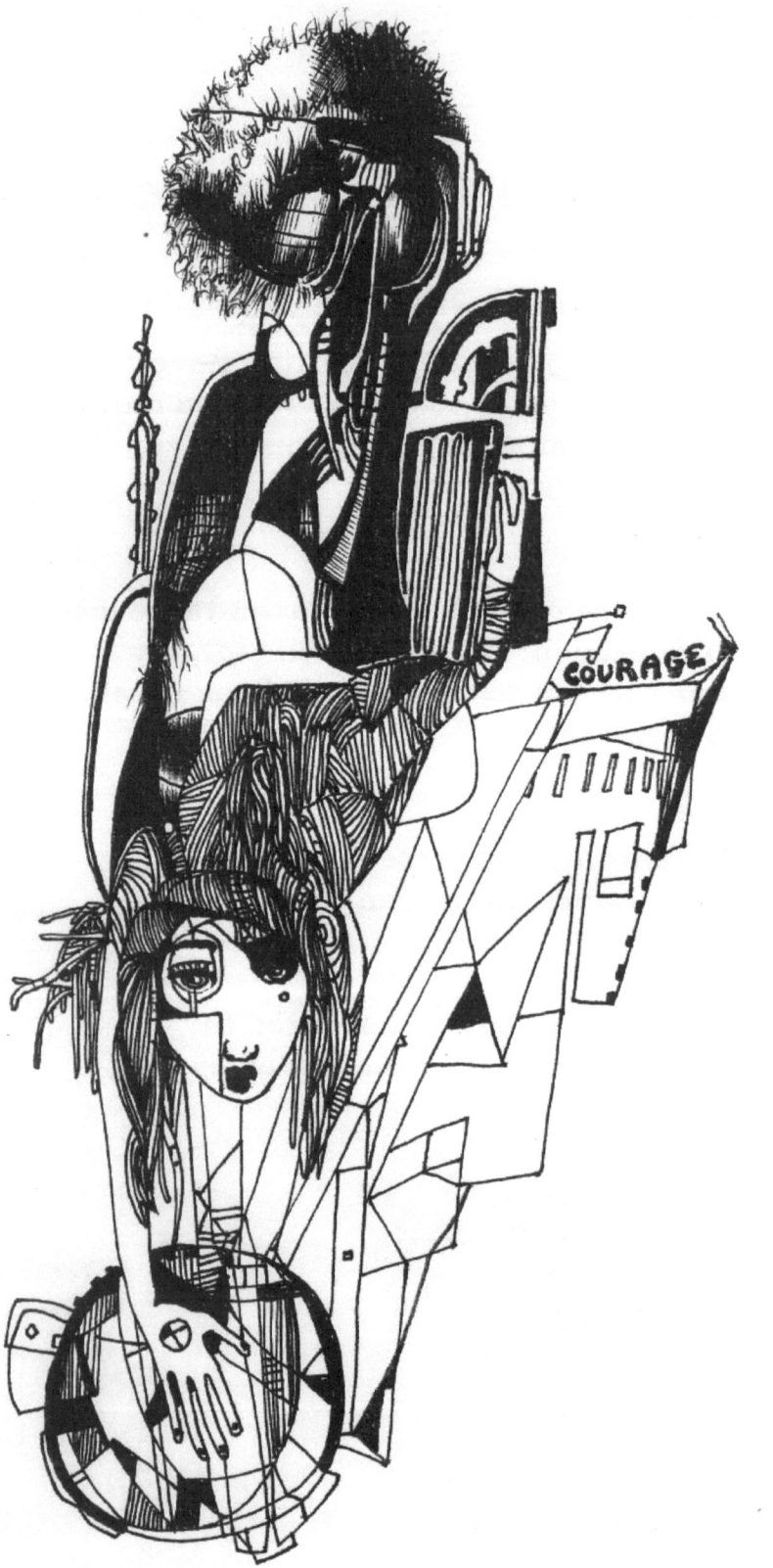

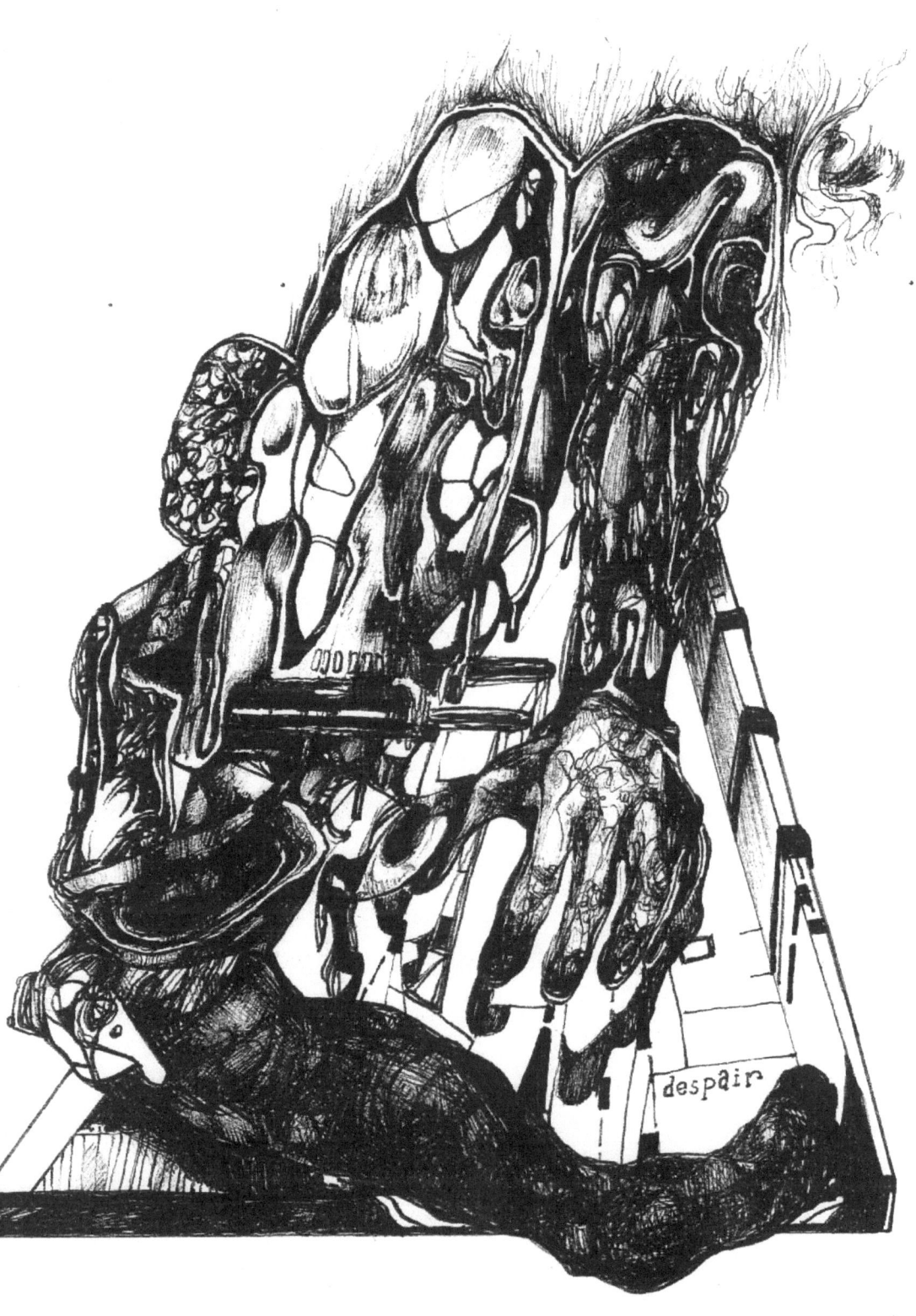

despair

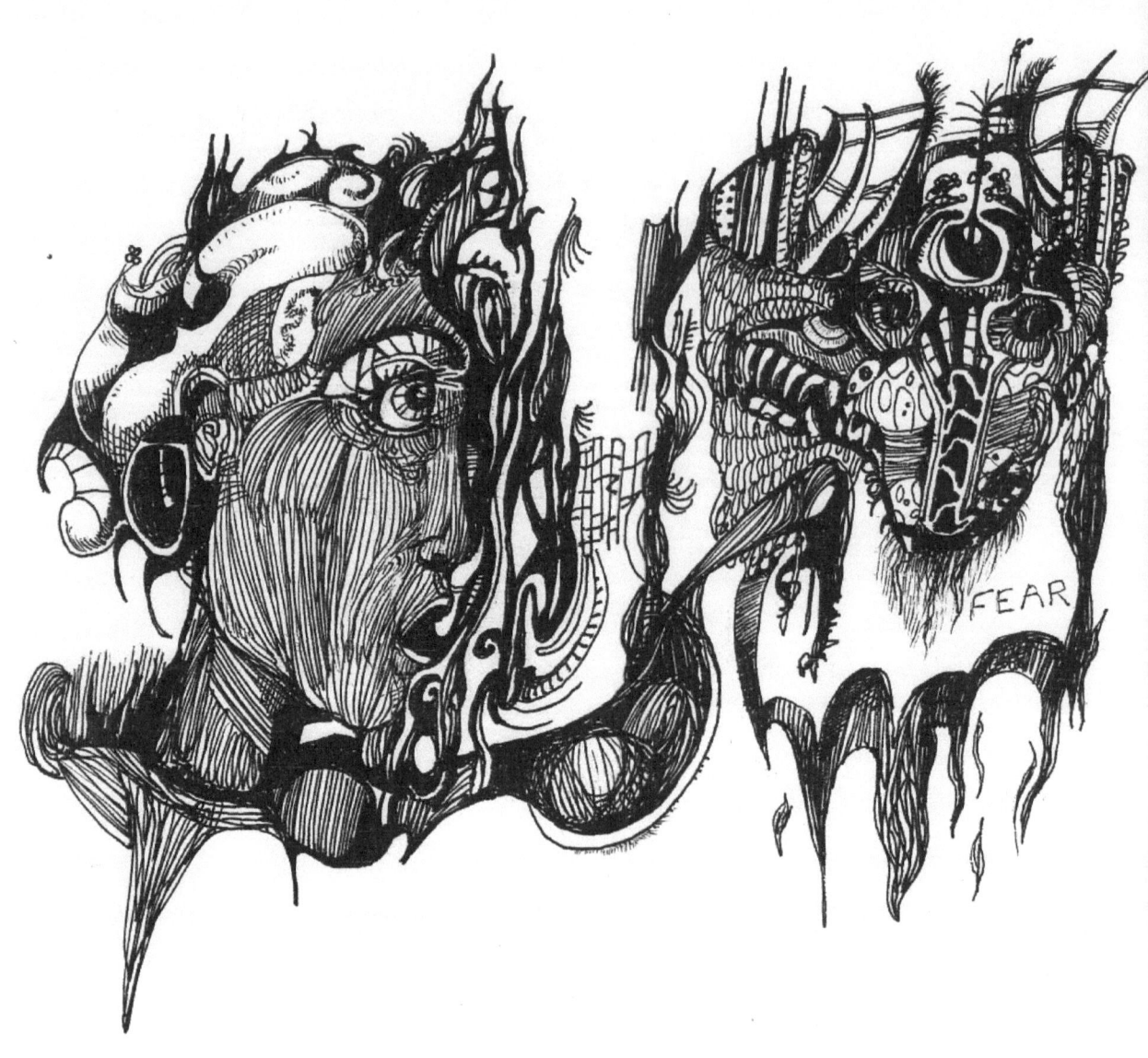

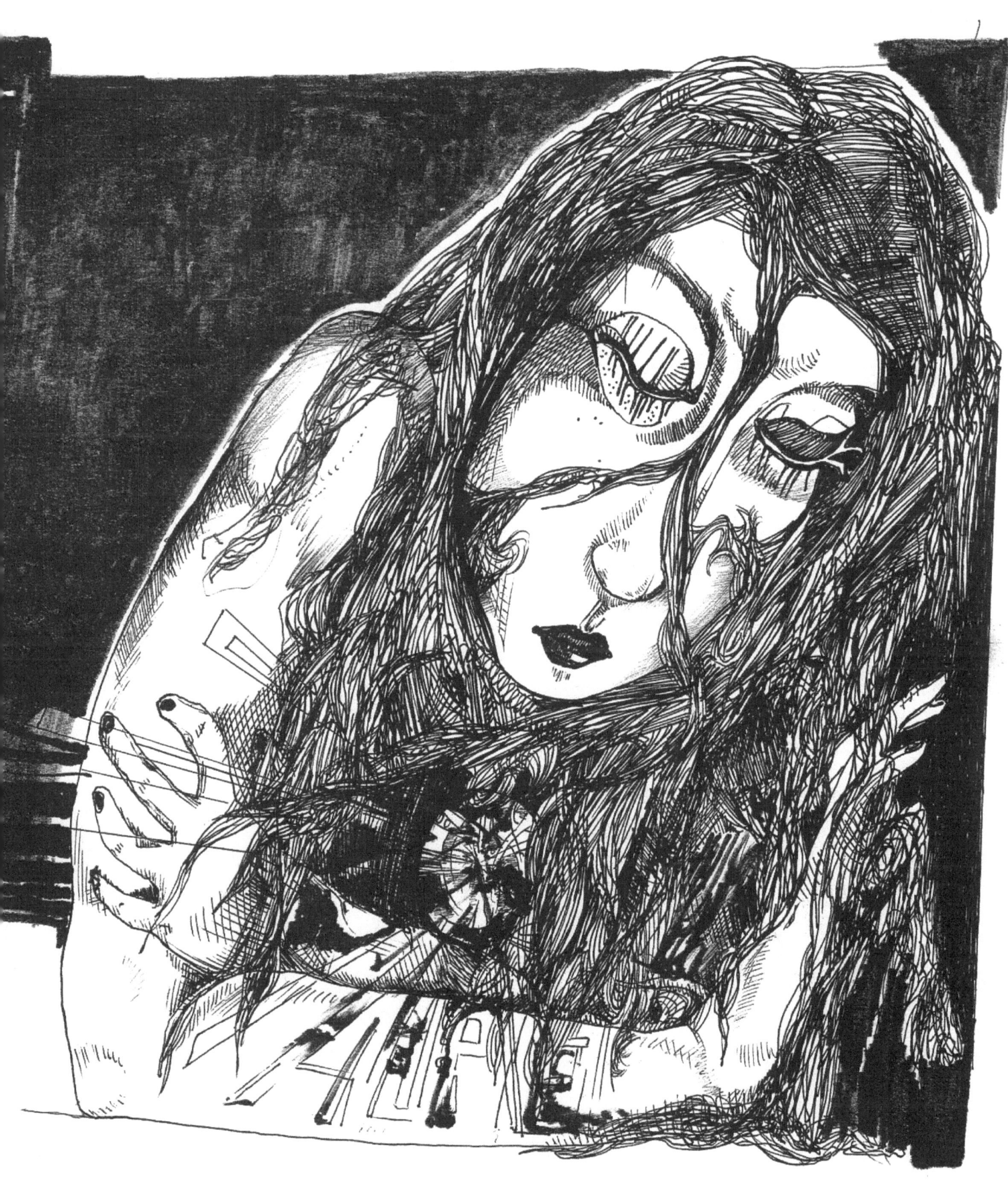

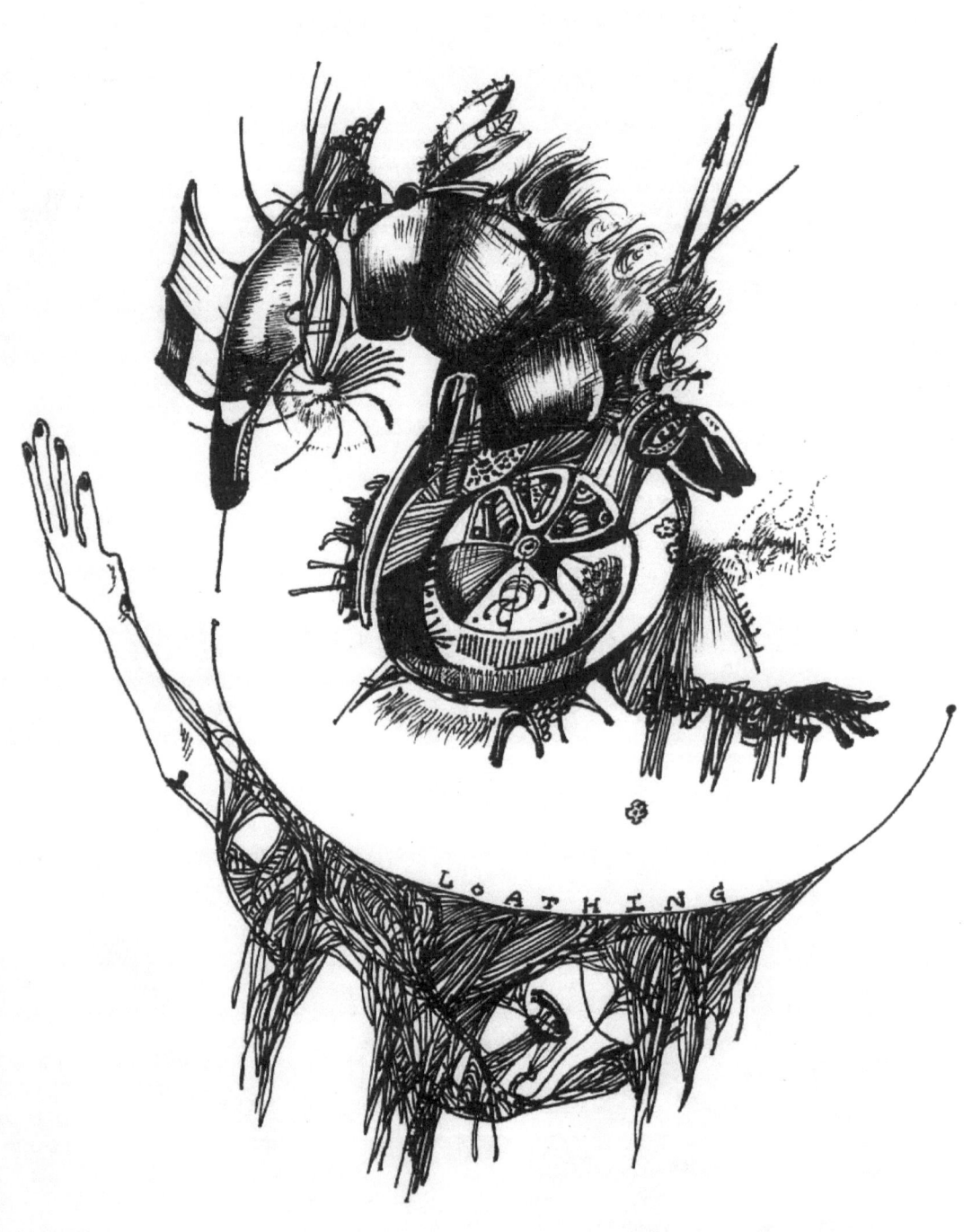

LOATHING

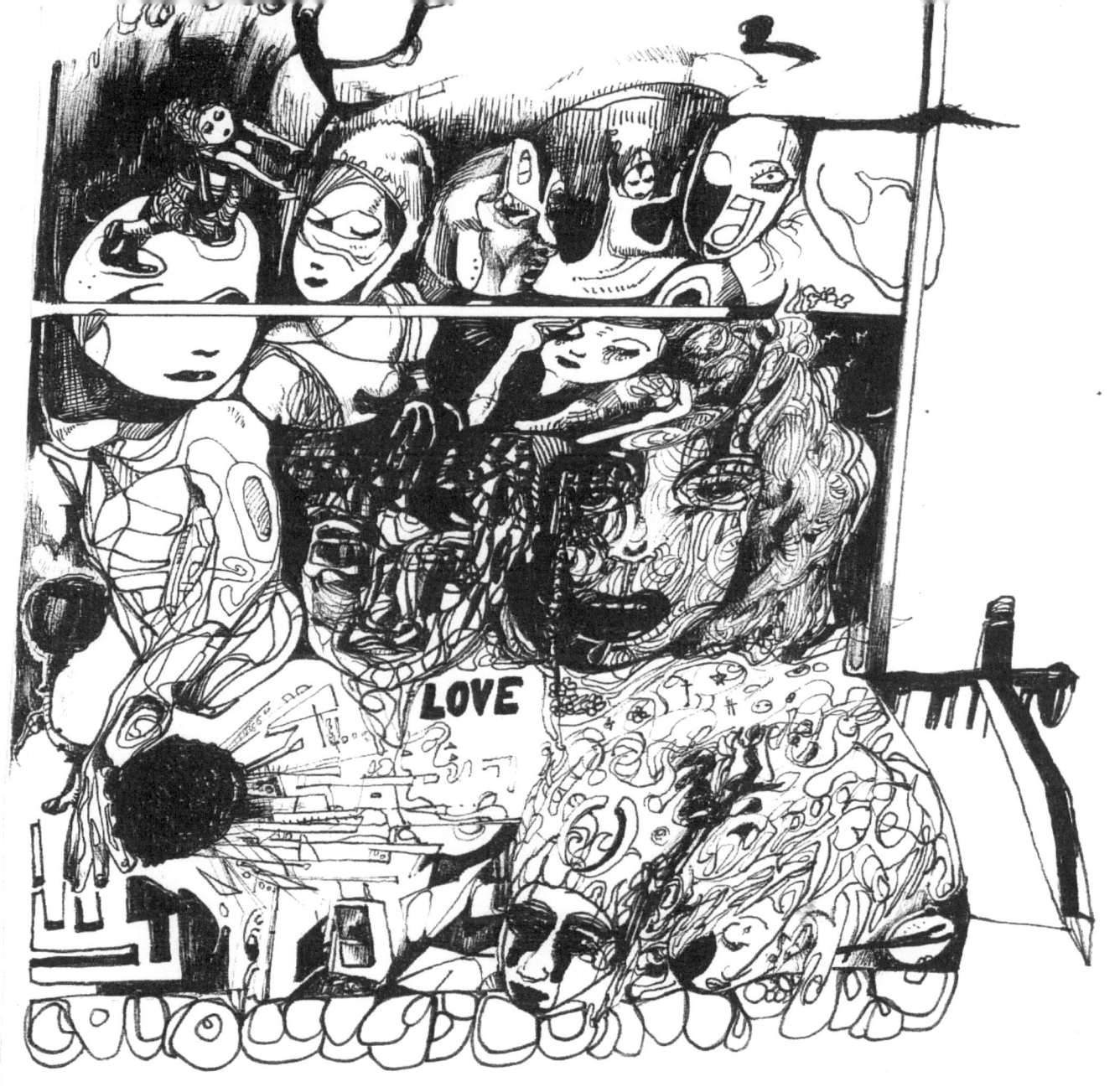

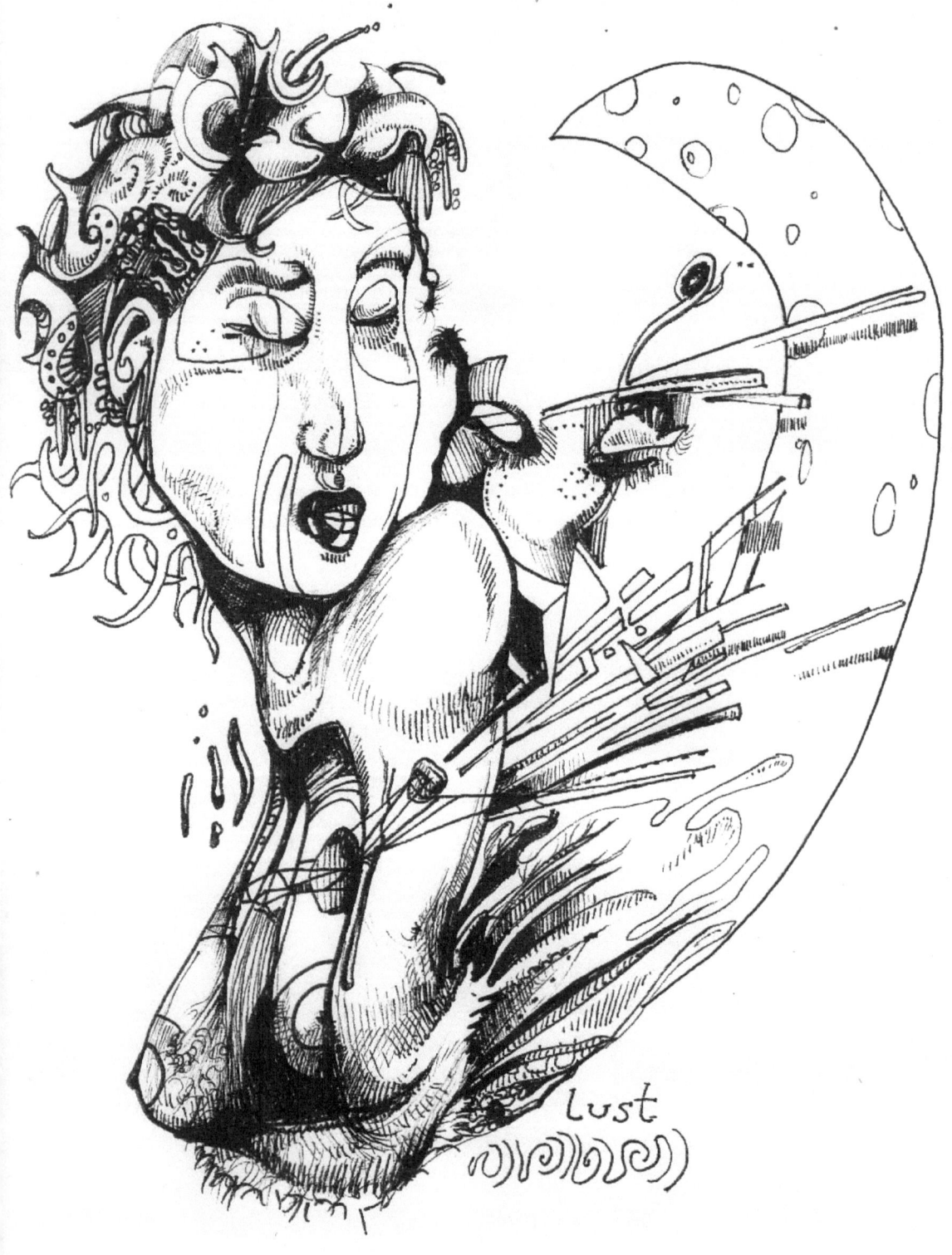

Lust

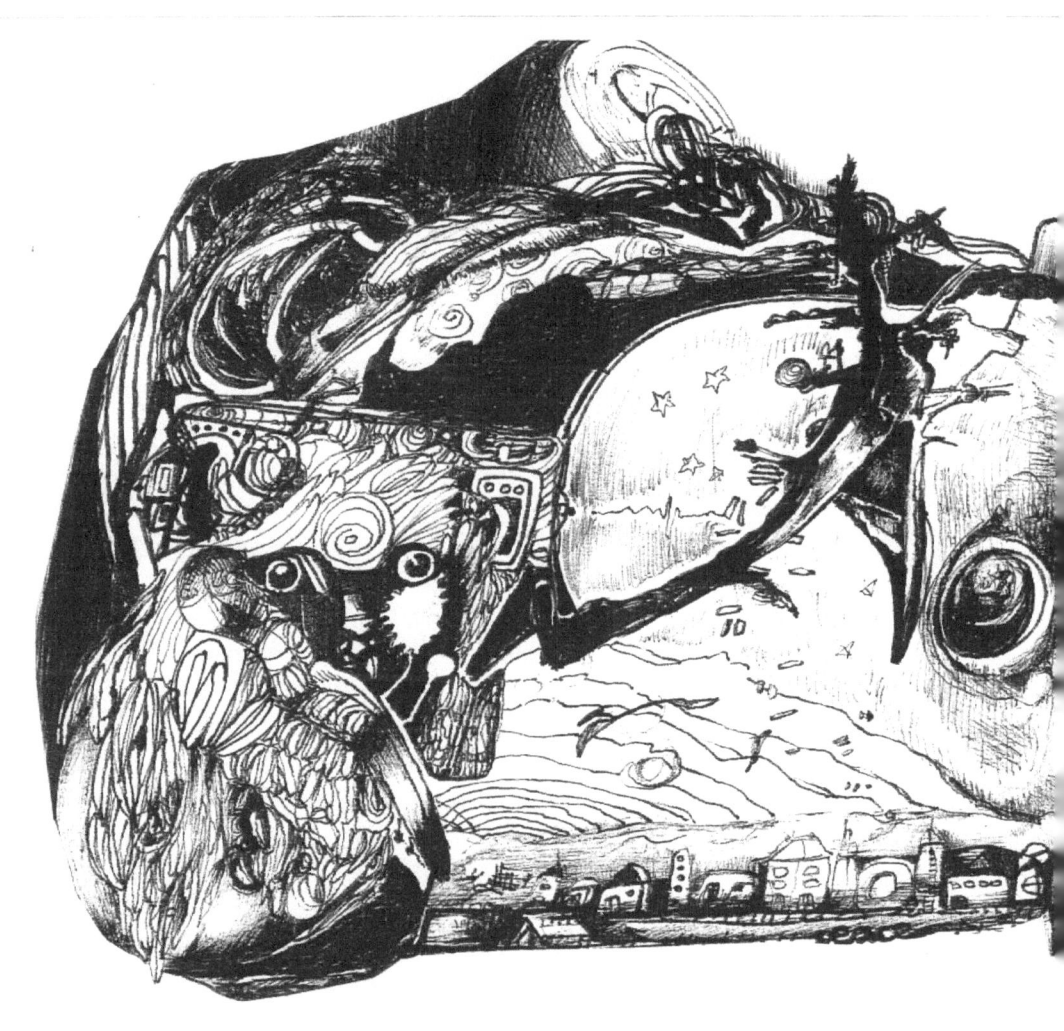

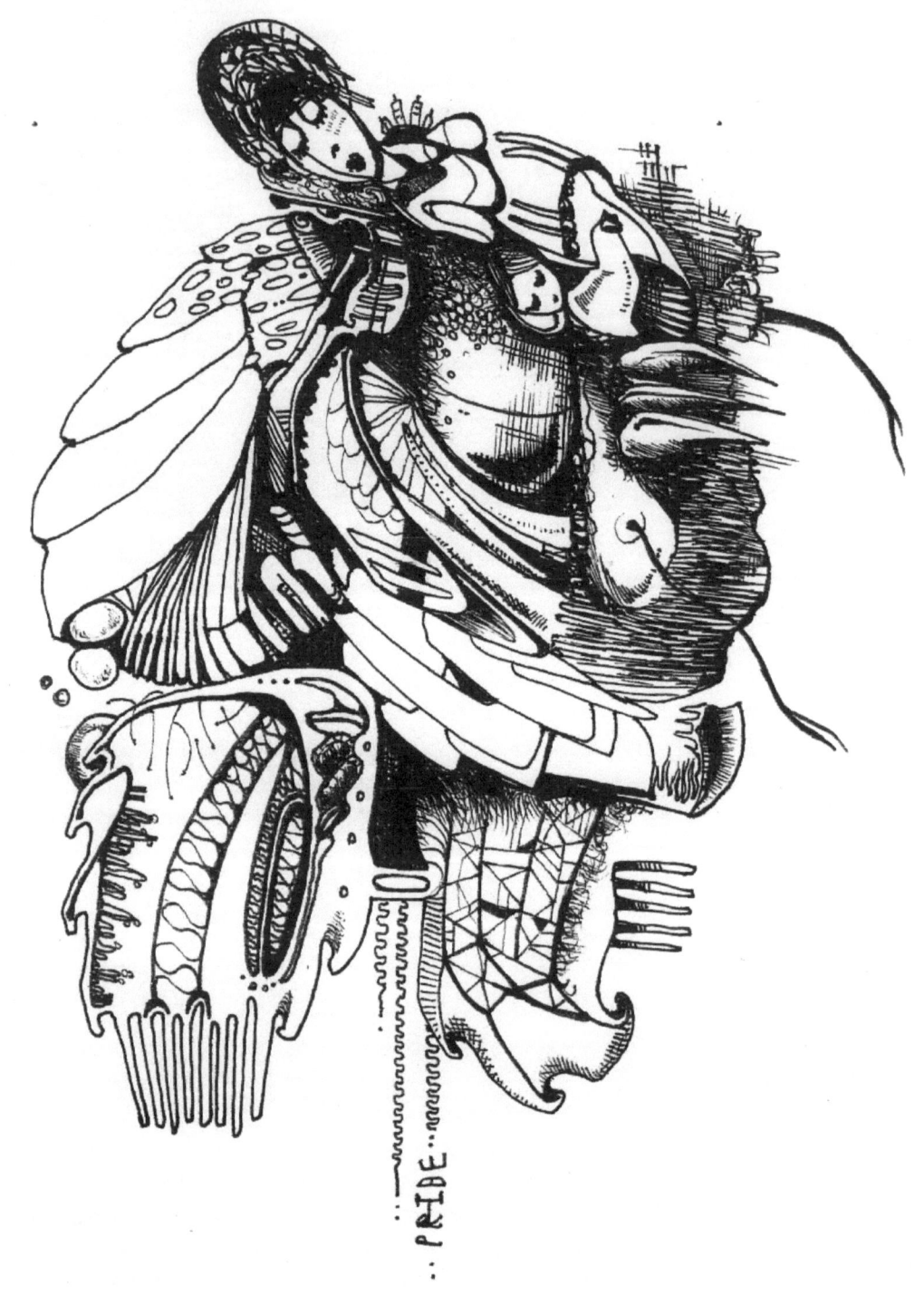

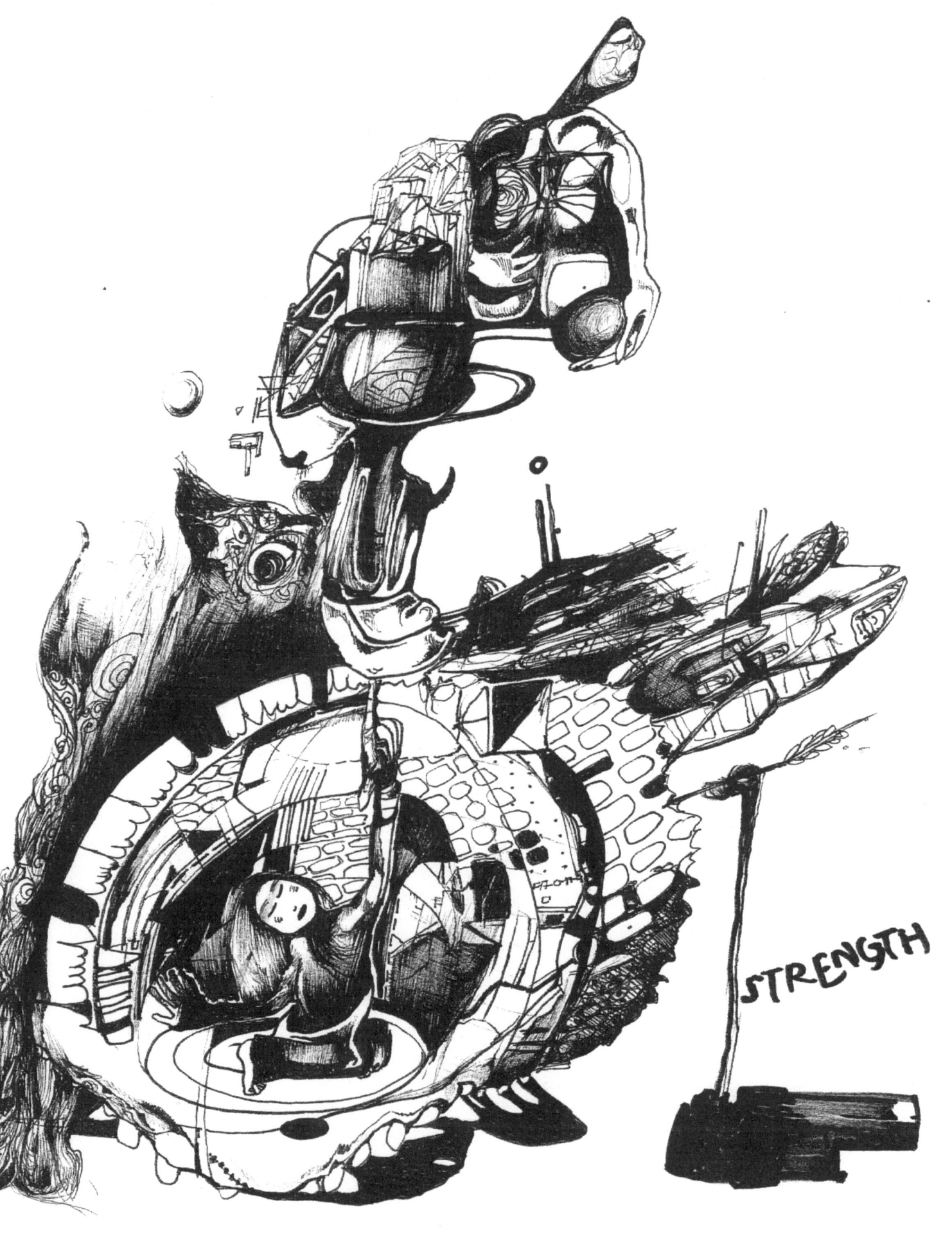

STRENGTH

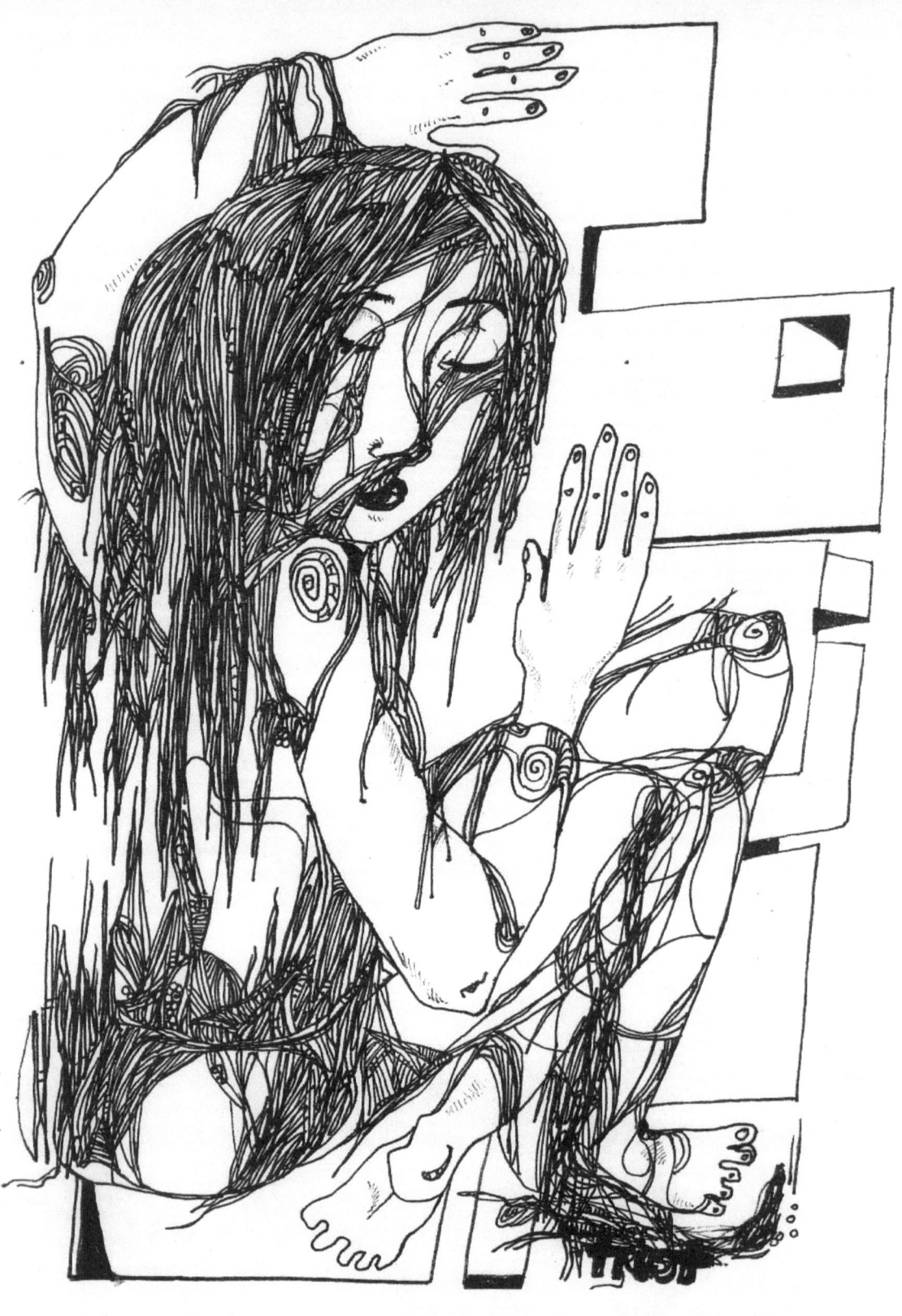

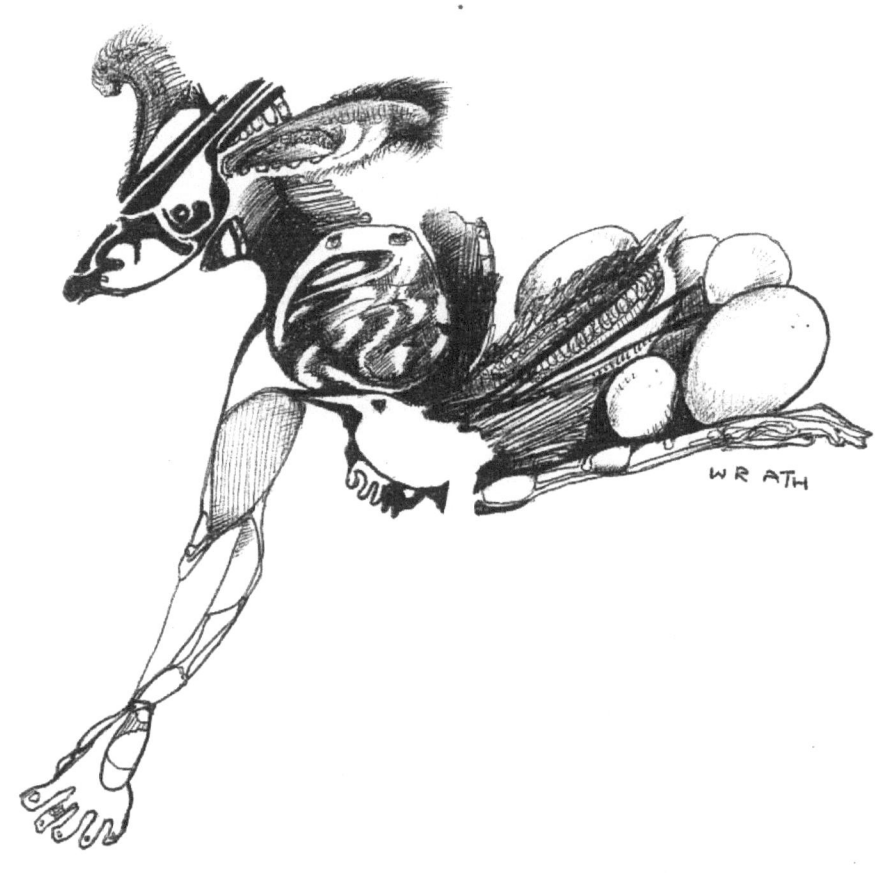

WR ATH

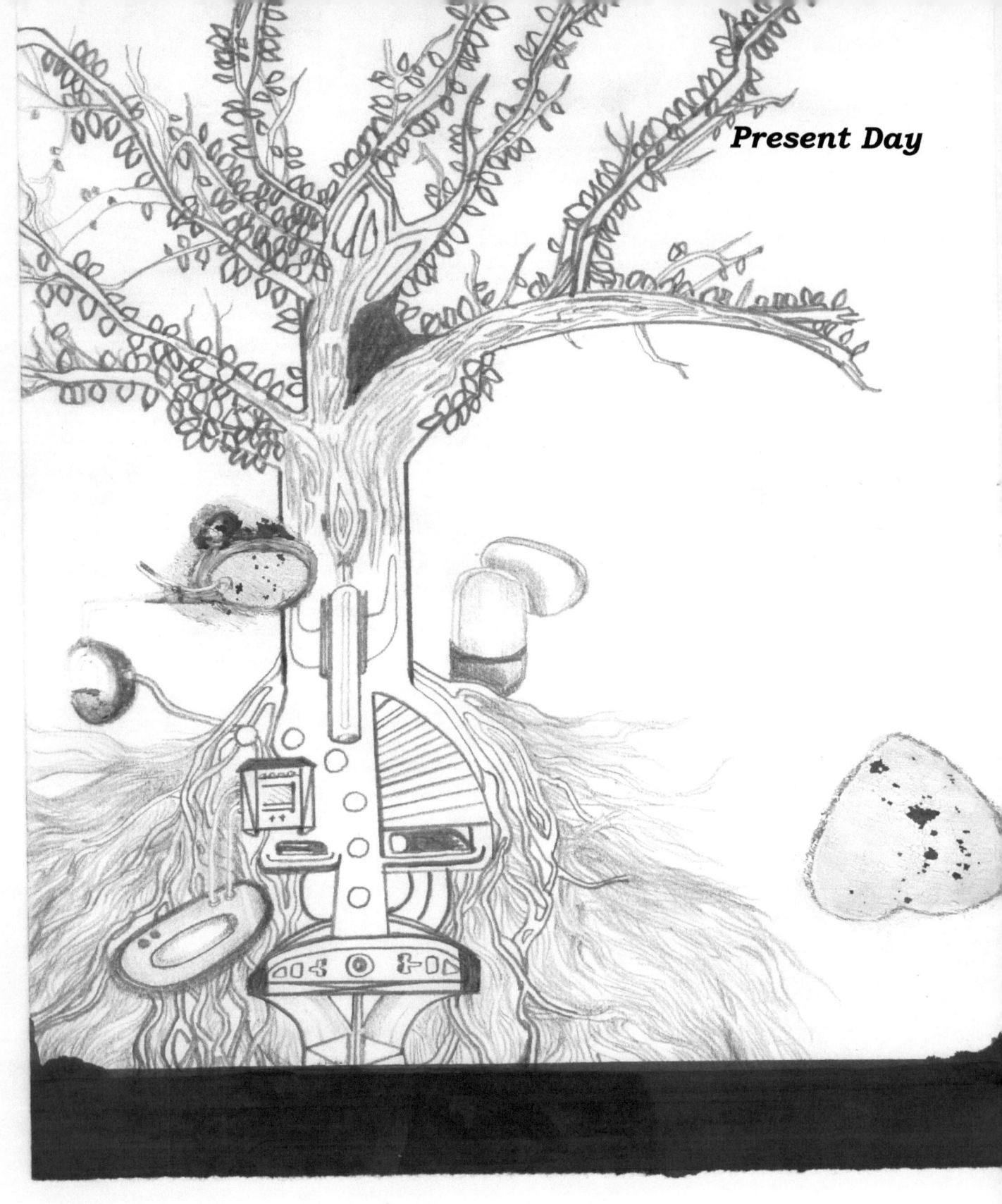

Mechanical Tree

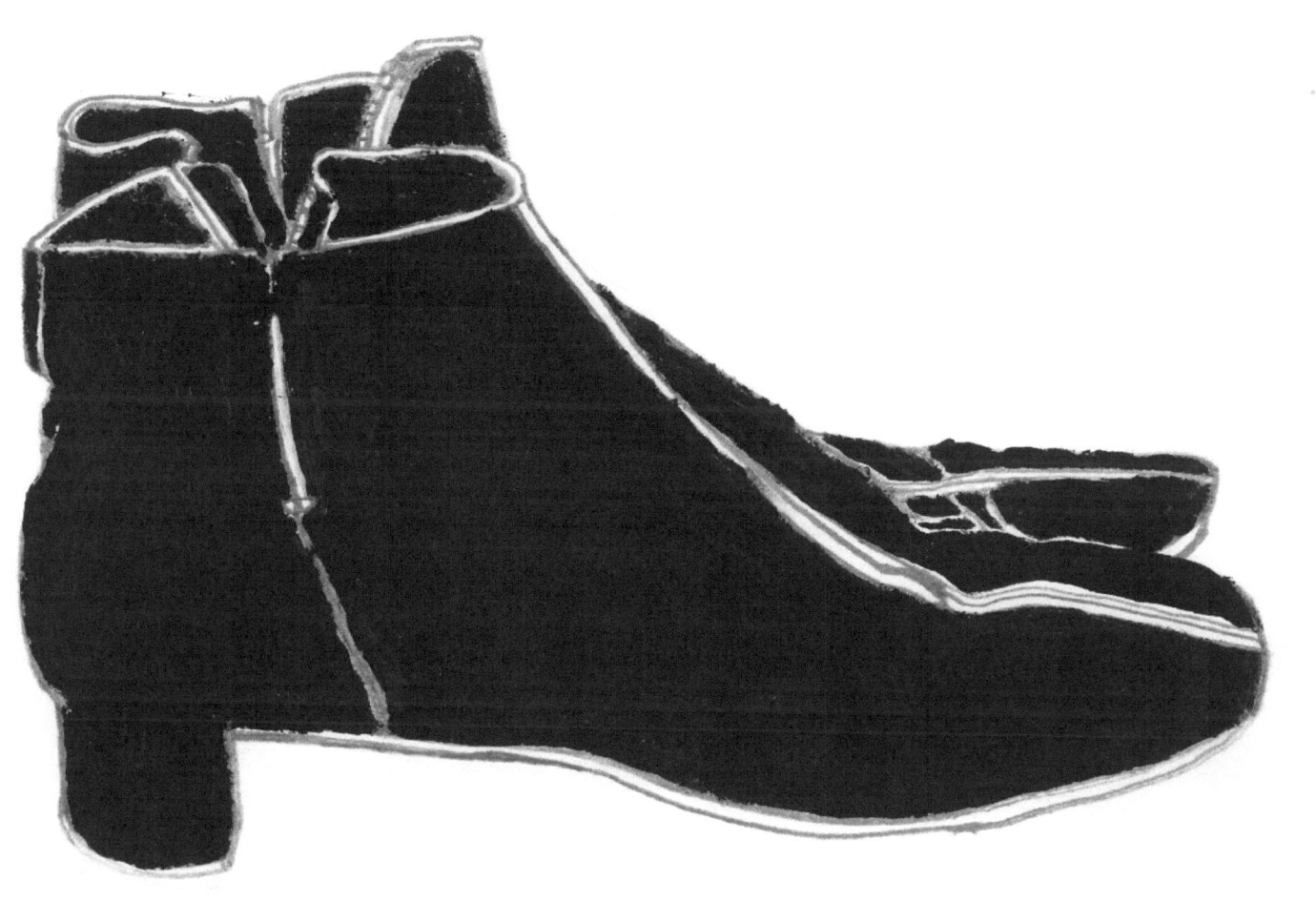

Boots

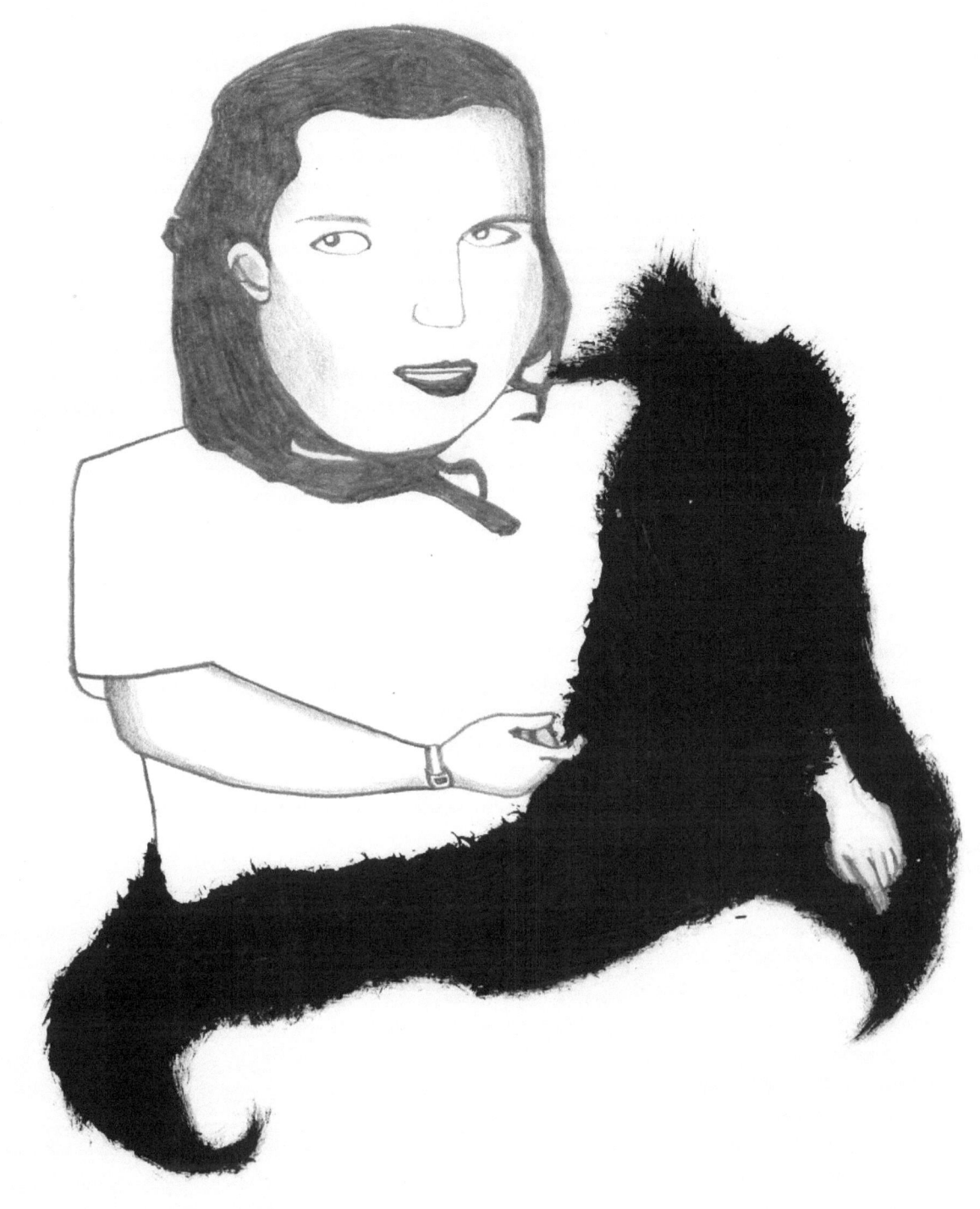

Rose

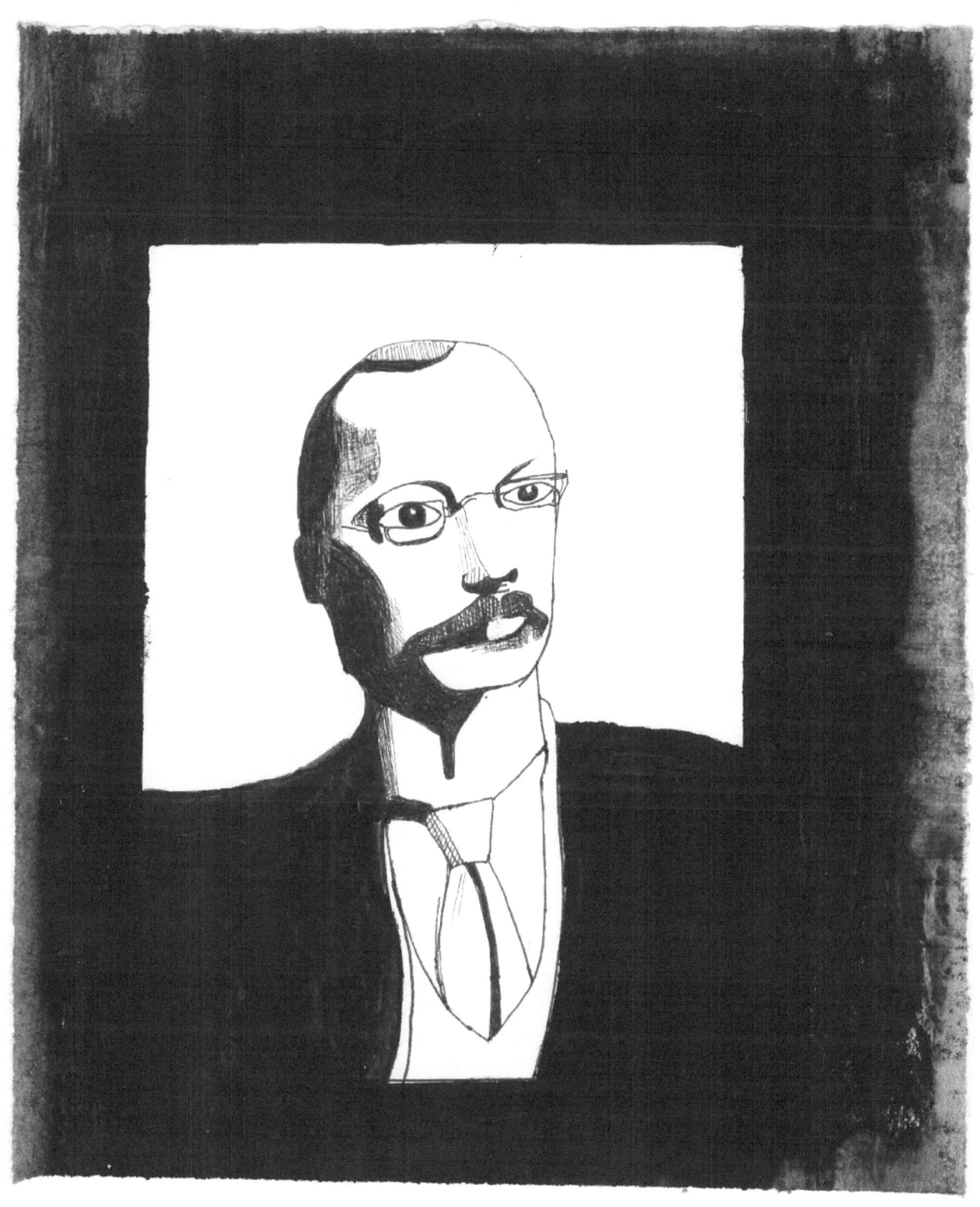

Doctor

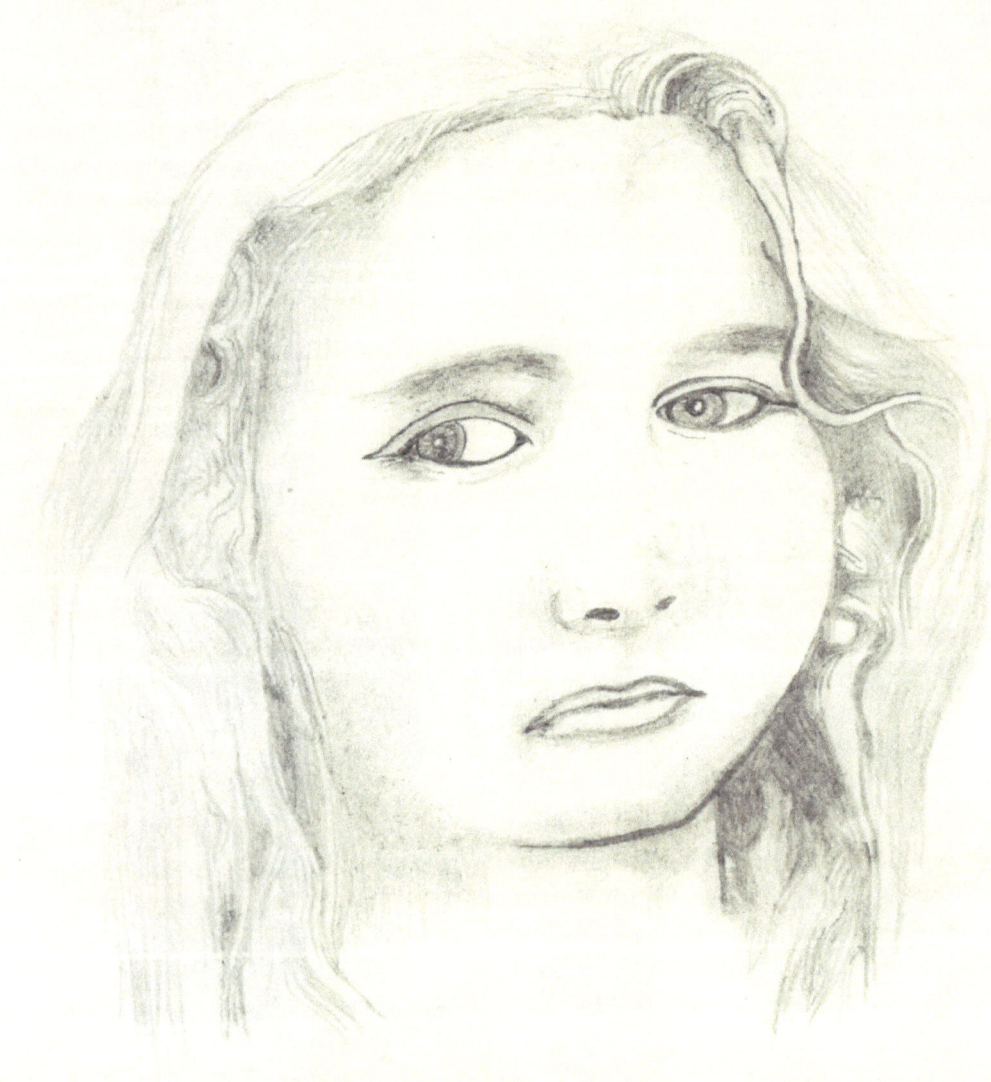

Louise

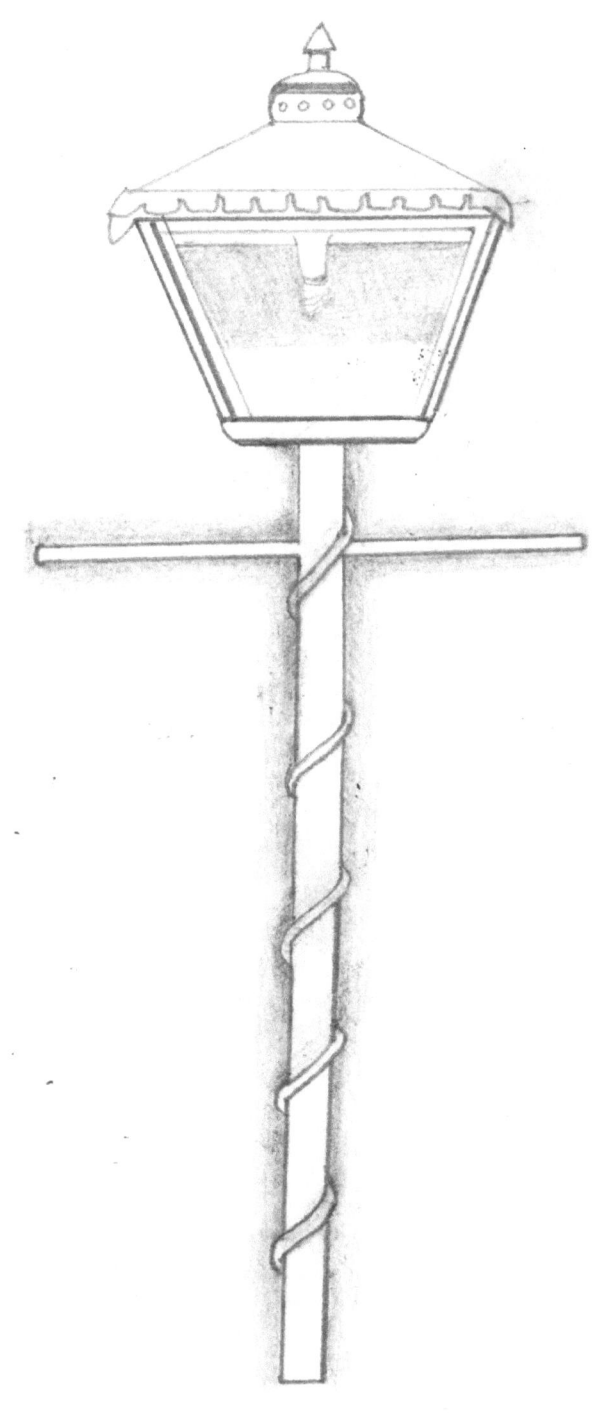

In the Garden

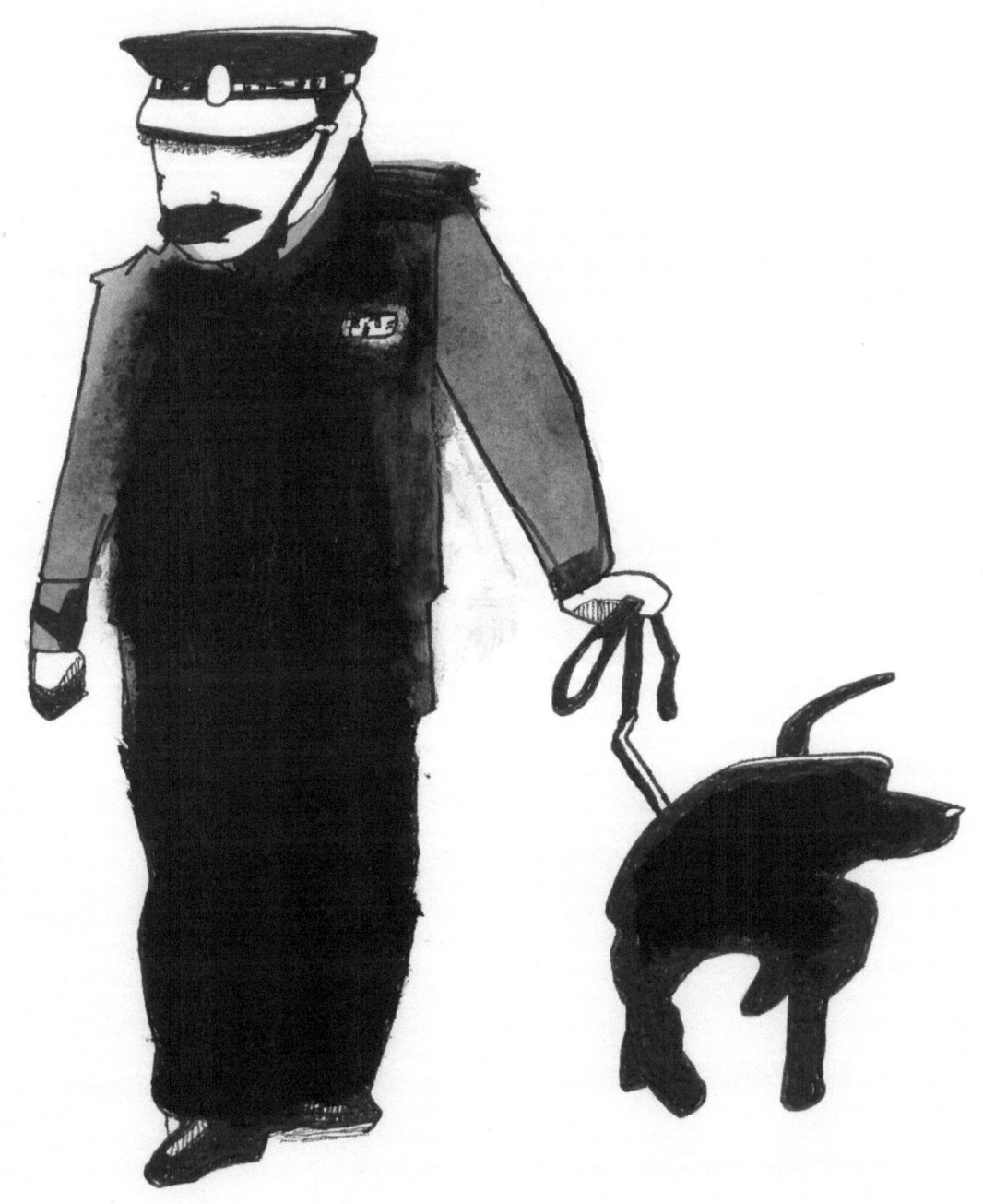

Police

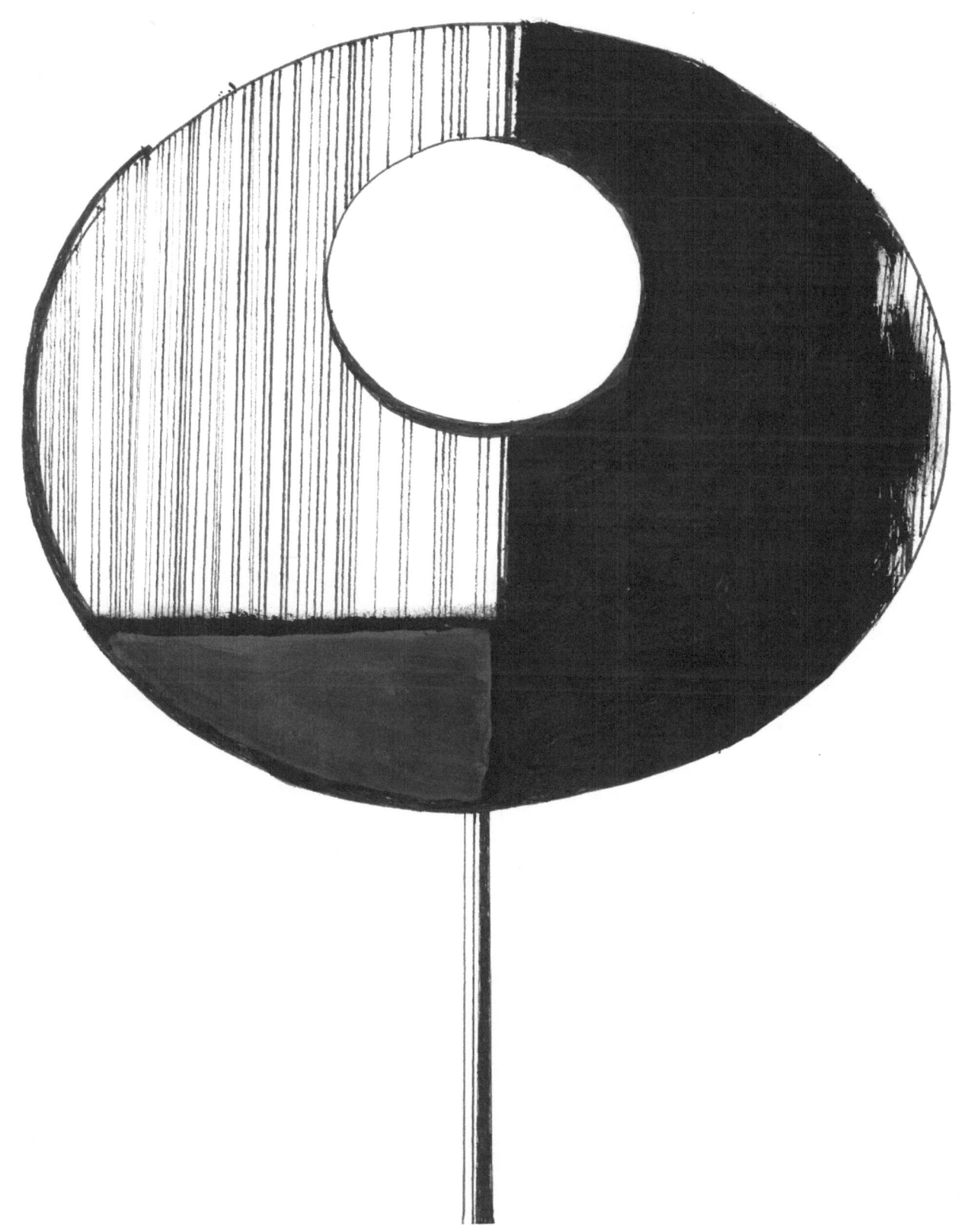

Abstract

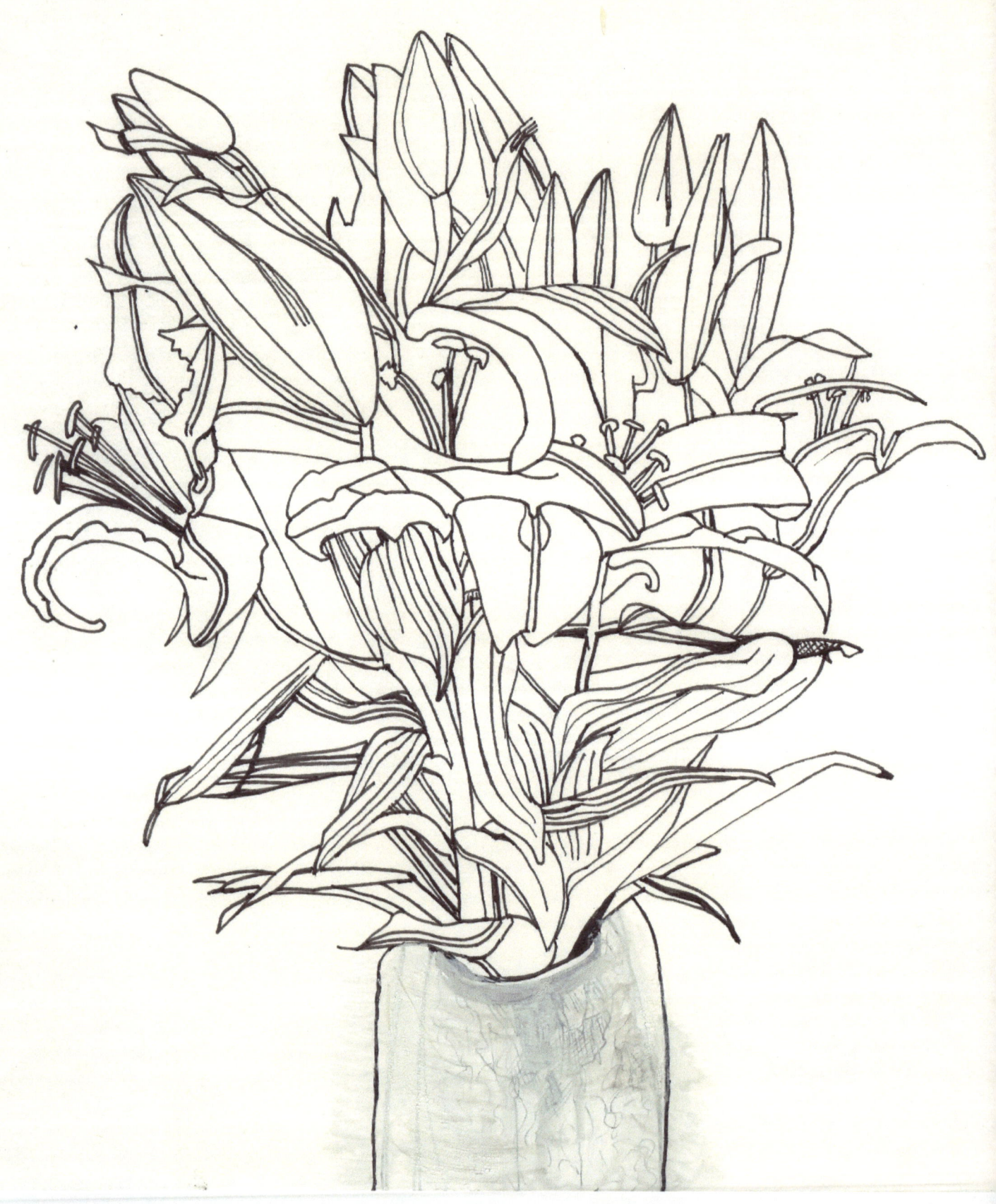

Flowers

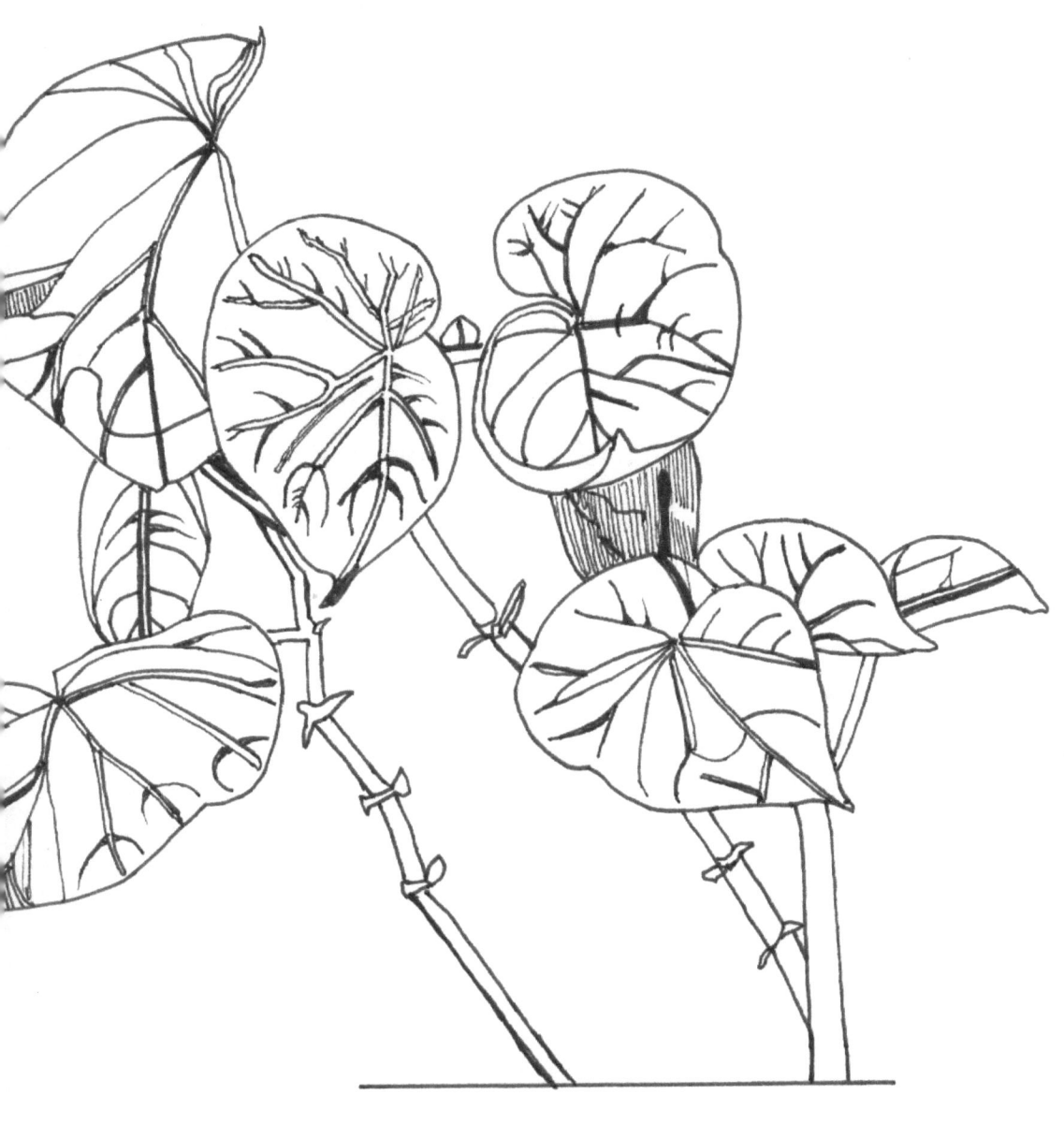

Plant Life

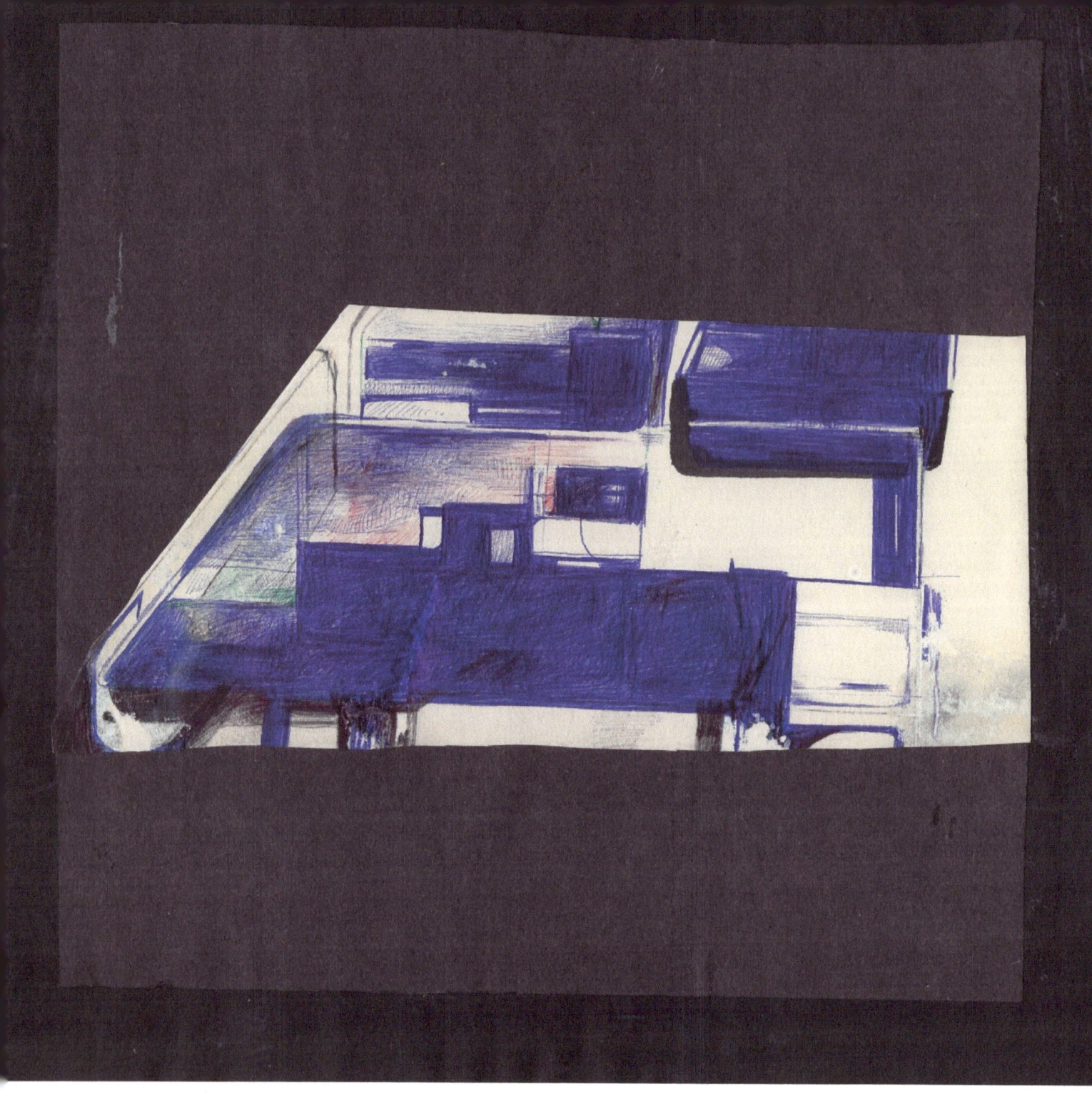

Glass Table

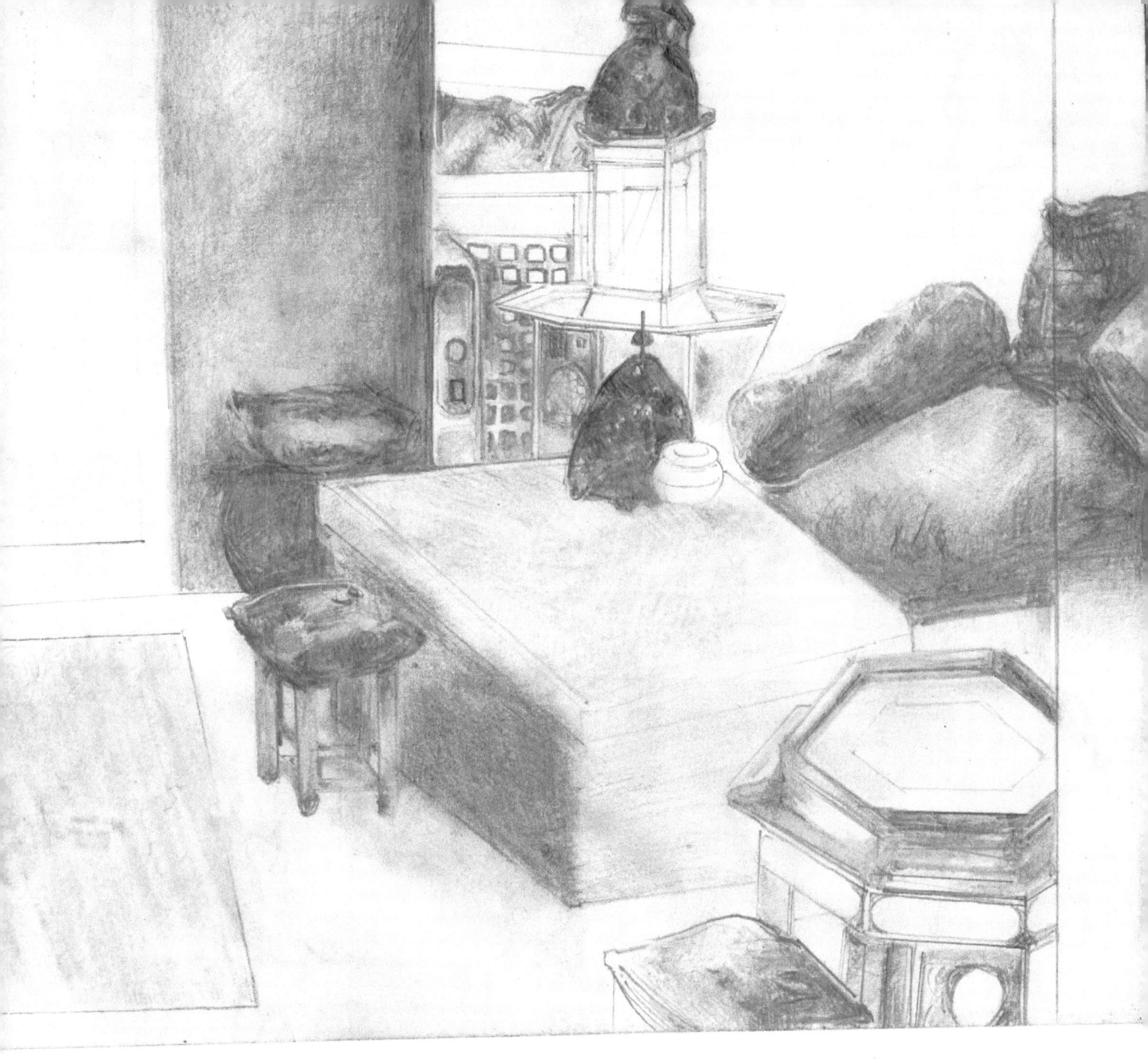

Camden Café

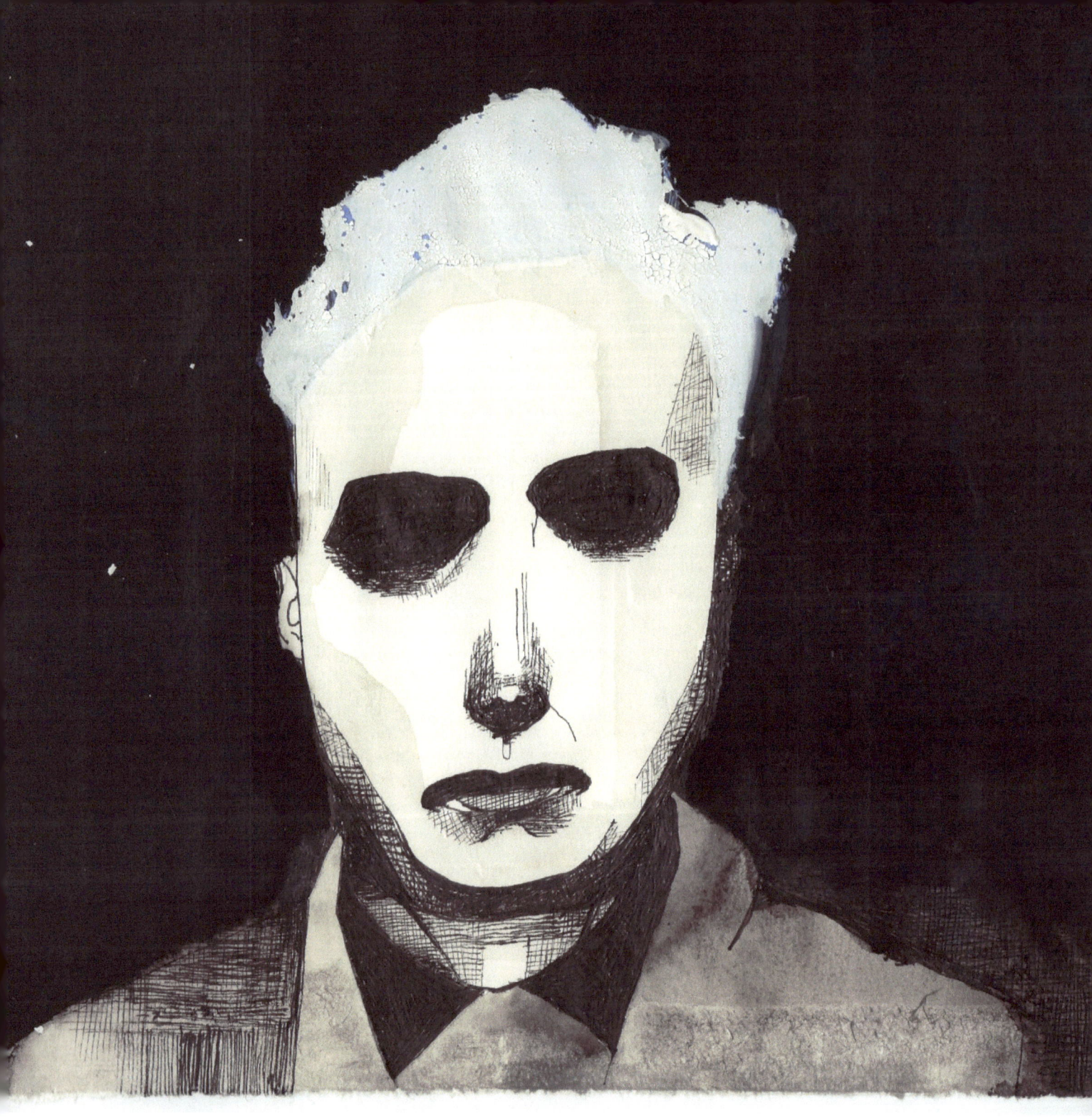

Haunted

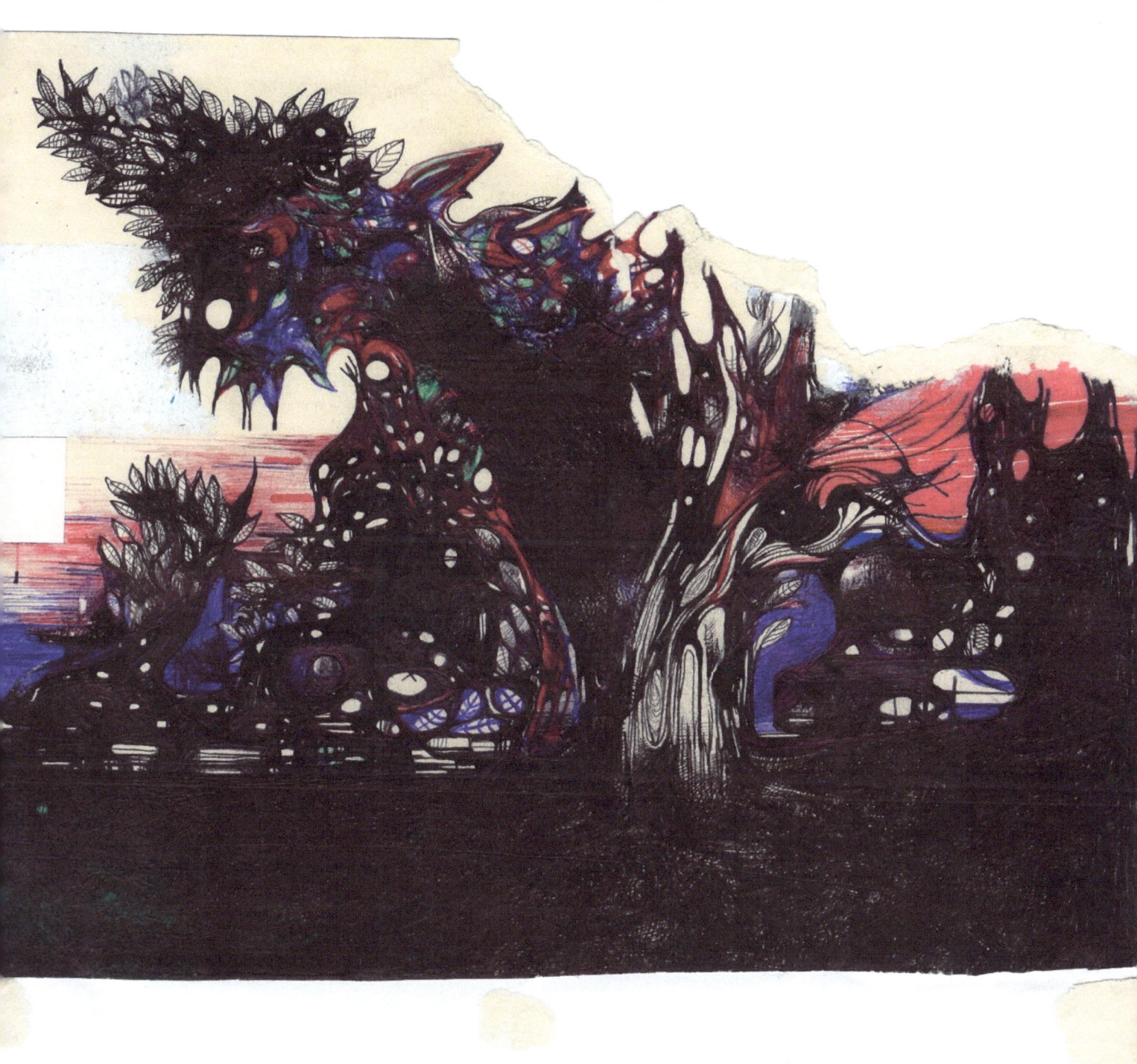

Dark Garden

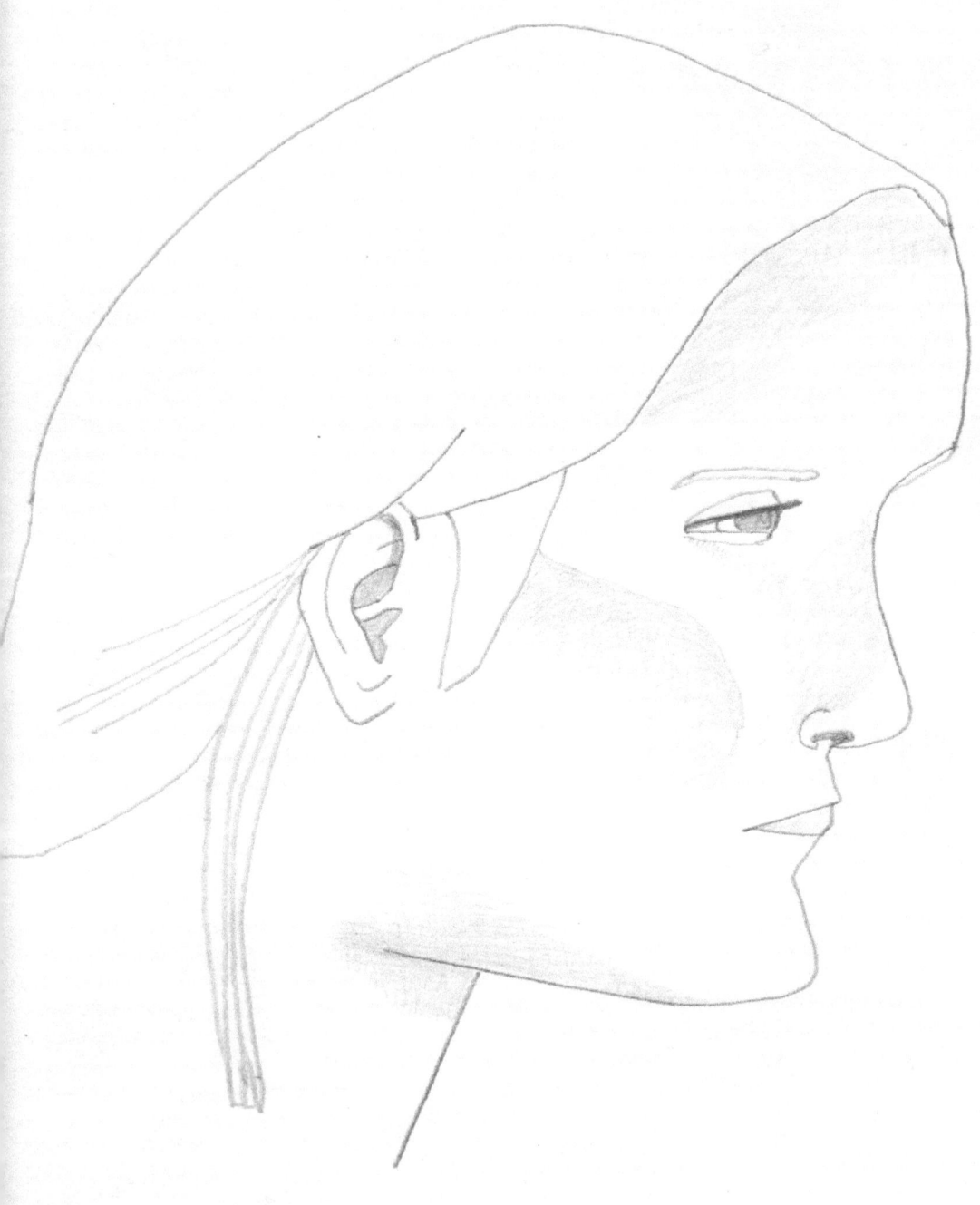

Carla

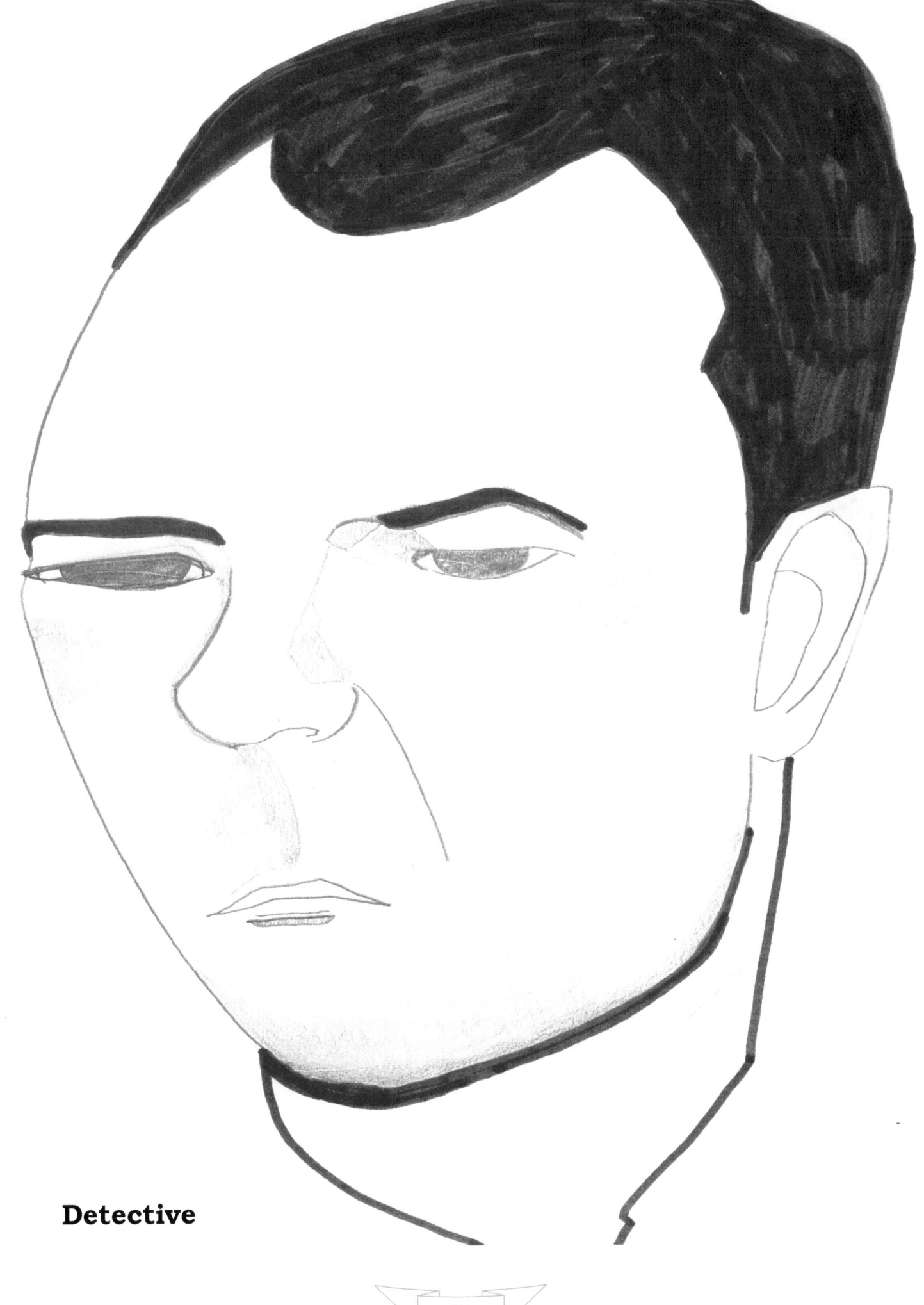

Detective

Mary Harrison

Mary Harrison was the mother of Louise and passed away in March 2002.

Mary was an author, broadcaster and artist.
Her paintings are presented on the following pages.

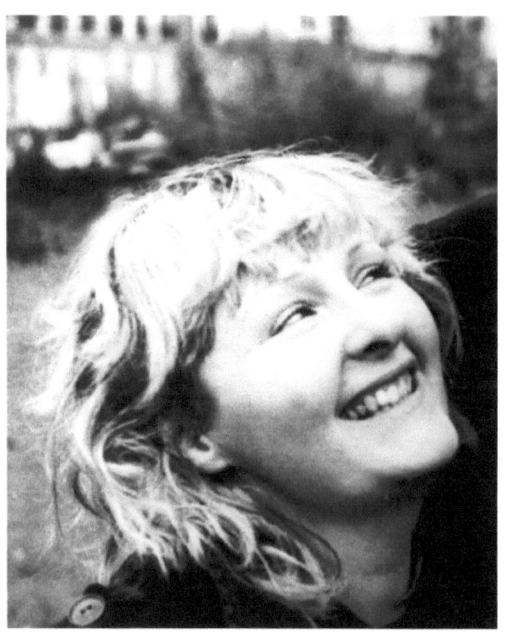

*I tidied Mary's grave today
The first time for a year
I placed a rose upon her cross
As I wiped away a tear*

Words: Laurence Harrison
Illustration: Louise Harrison

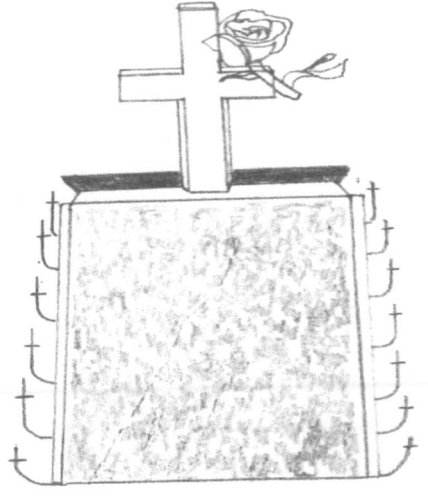

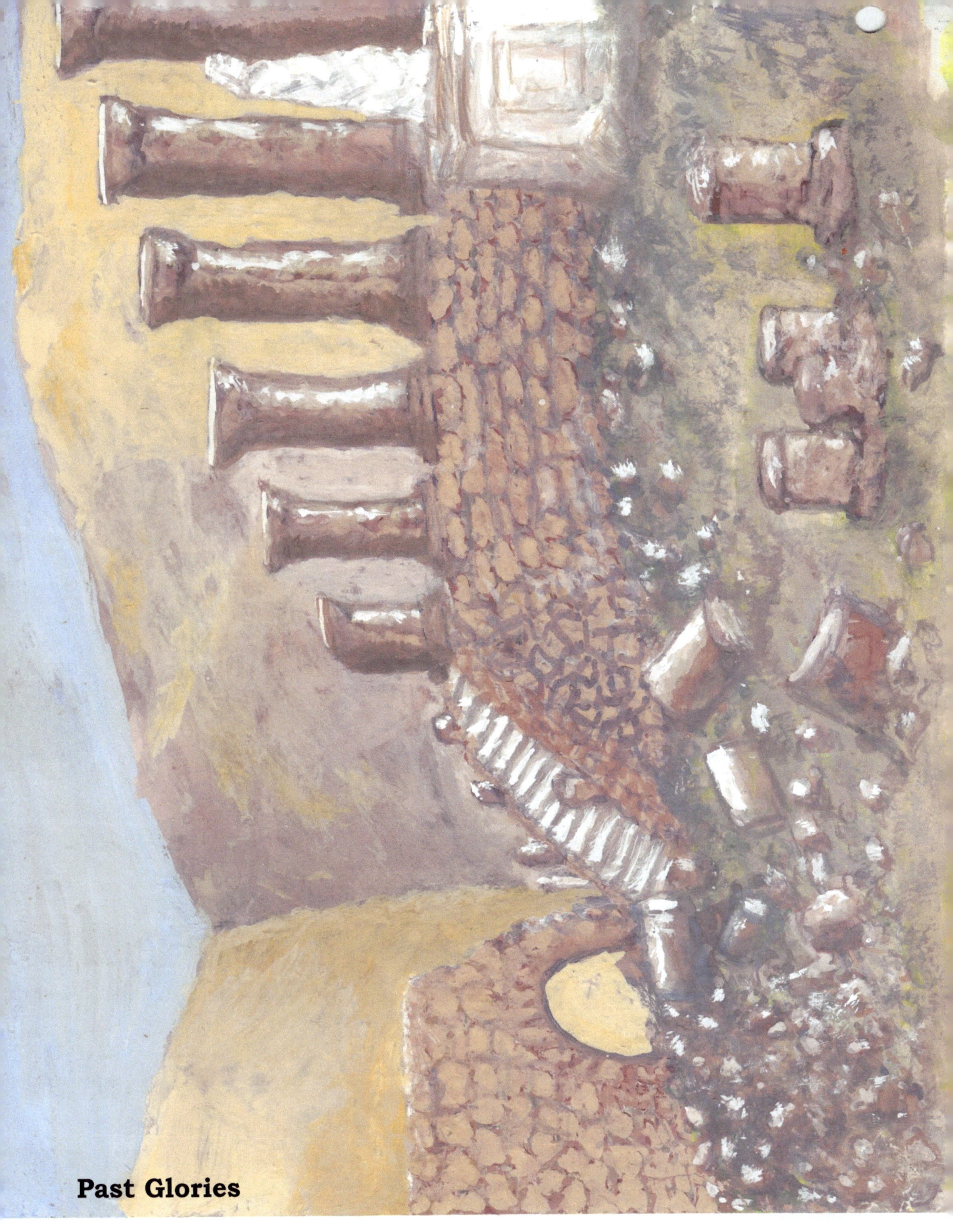

Past Glories

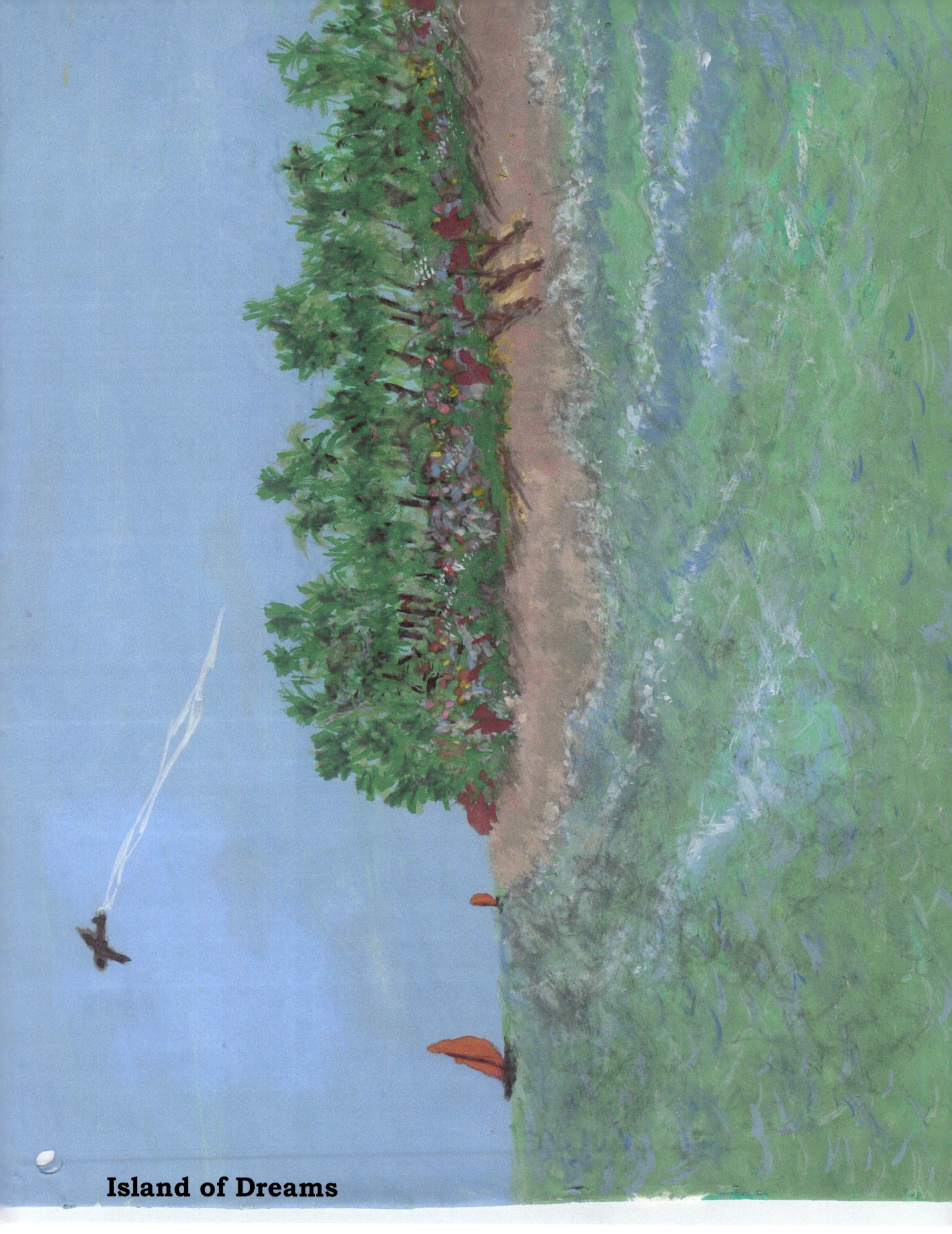

Island of Dreams

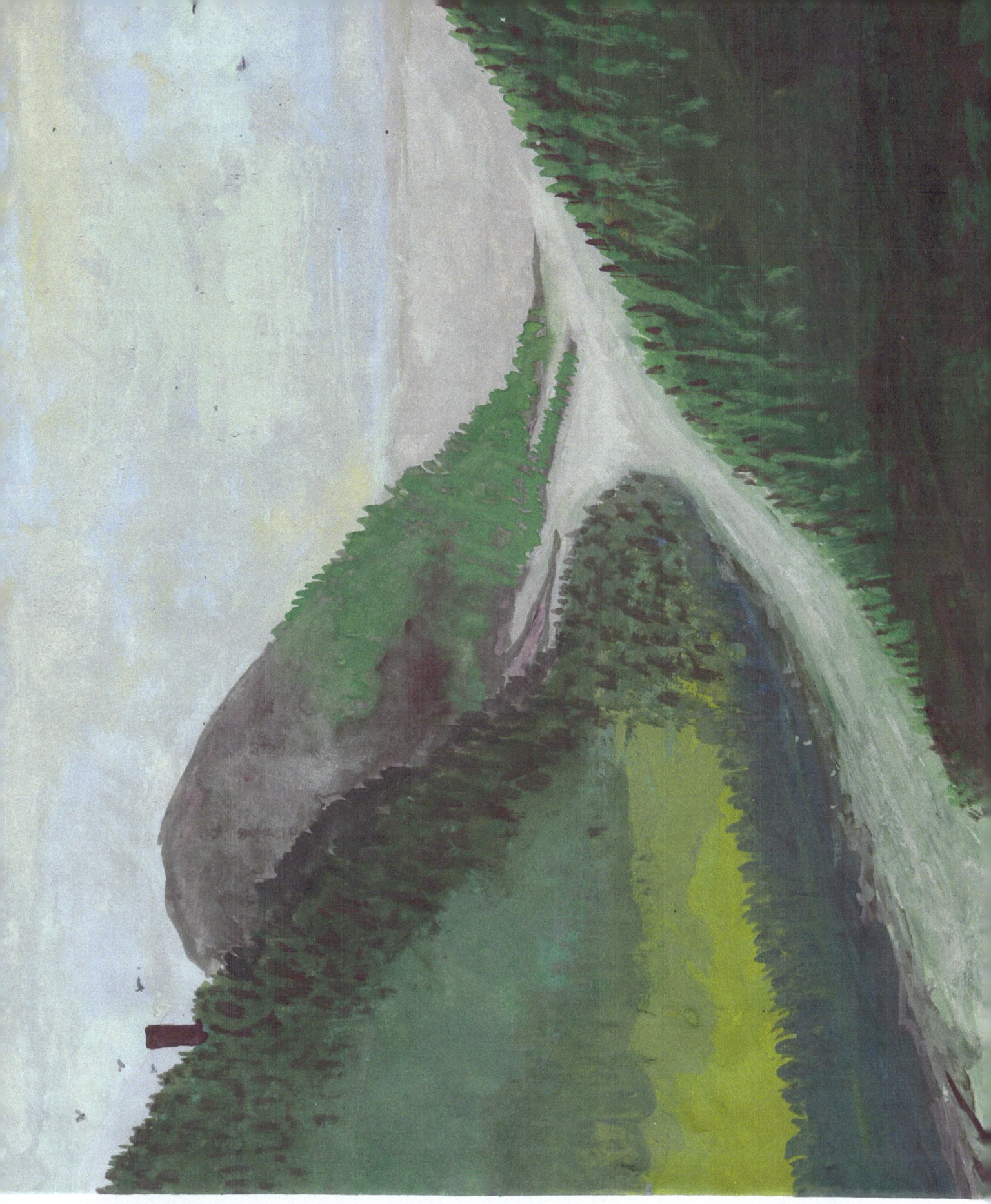

River Valley

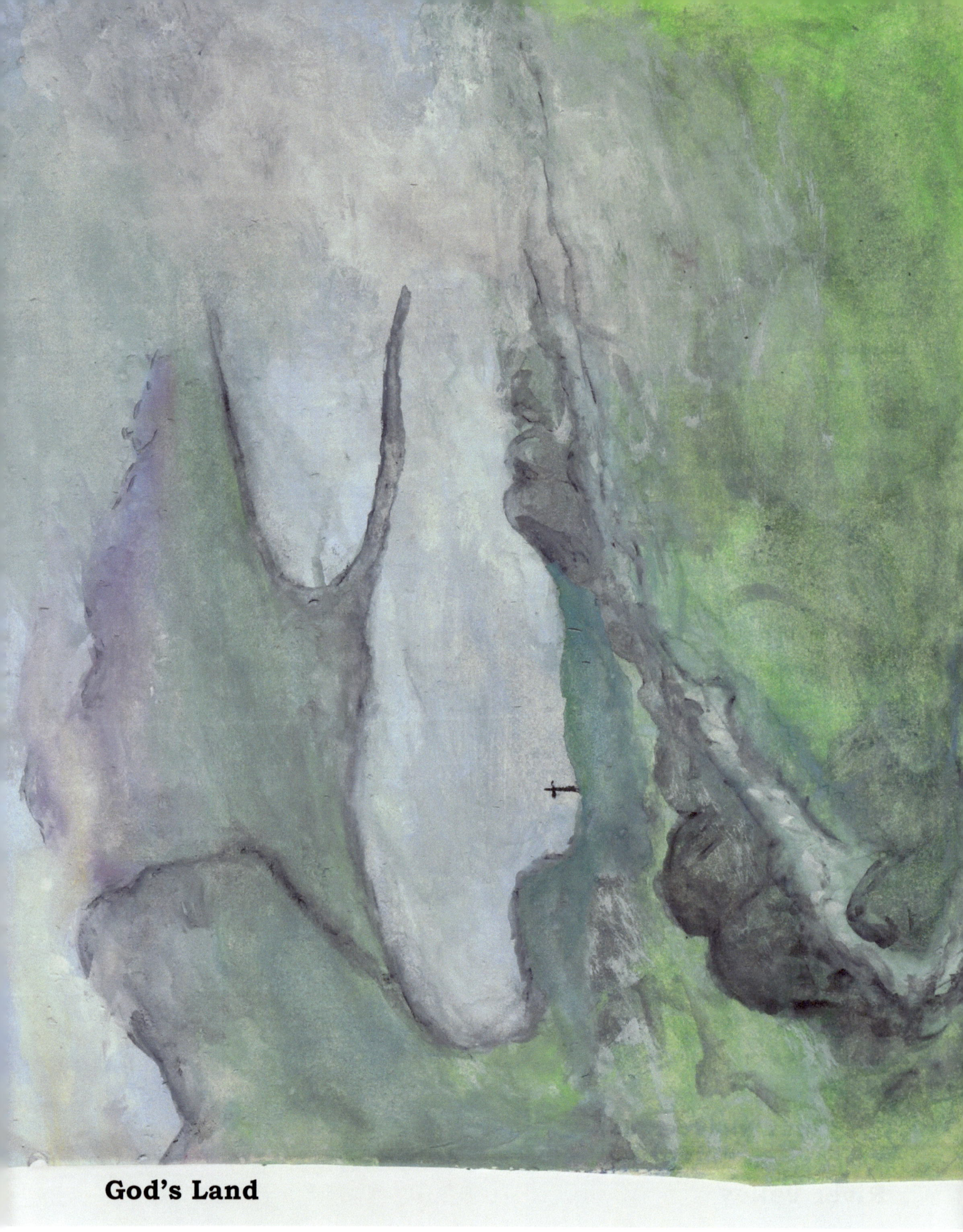

God's Land

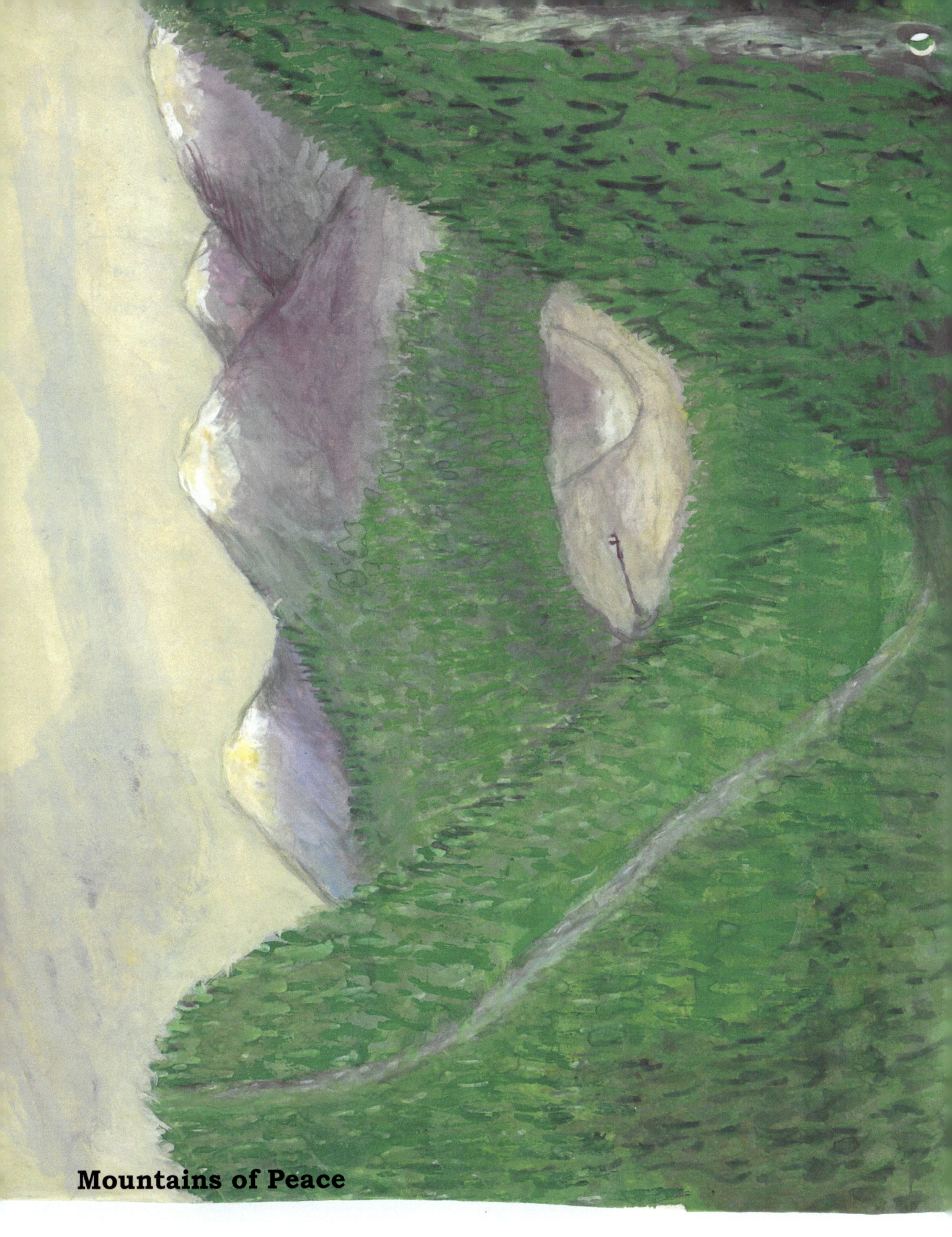

Mountains of Peace

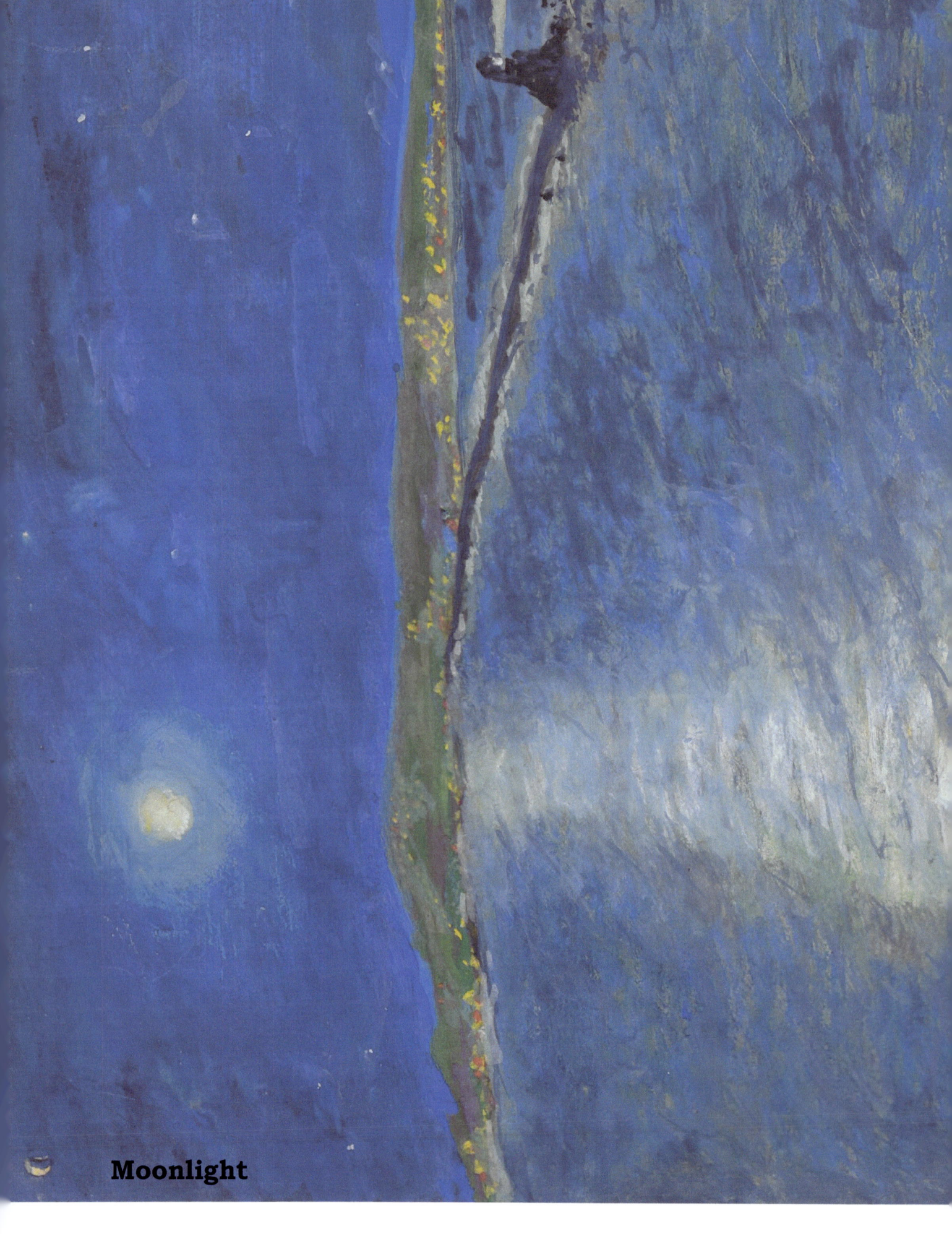

Moonlight

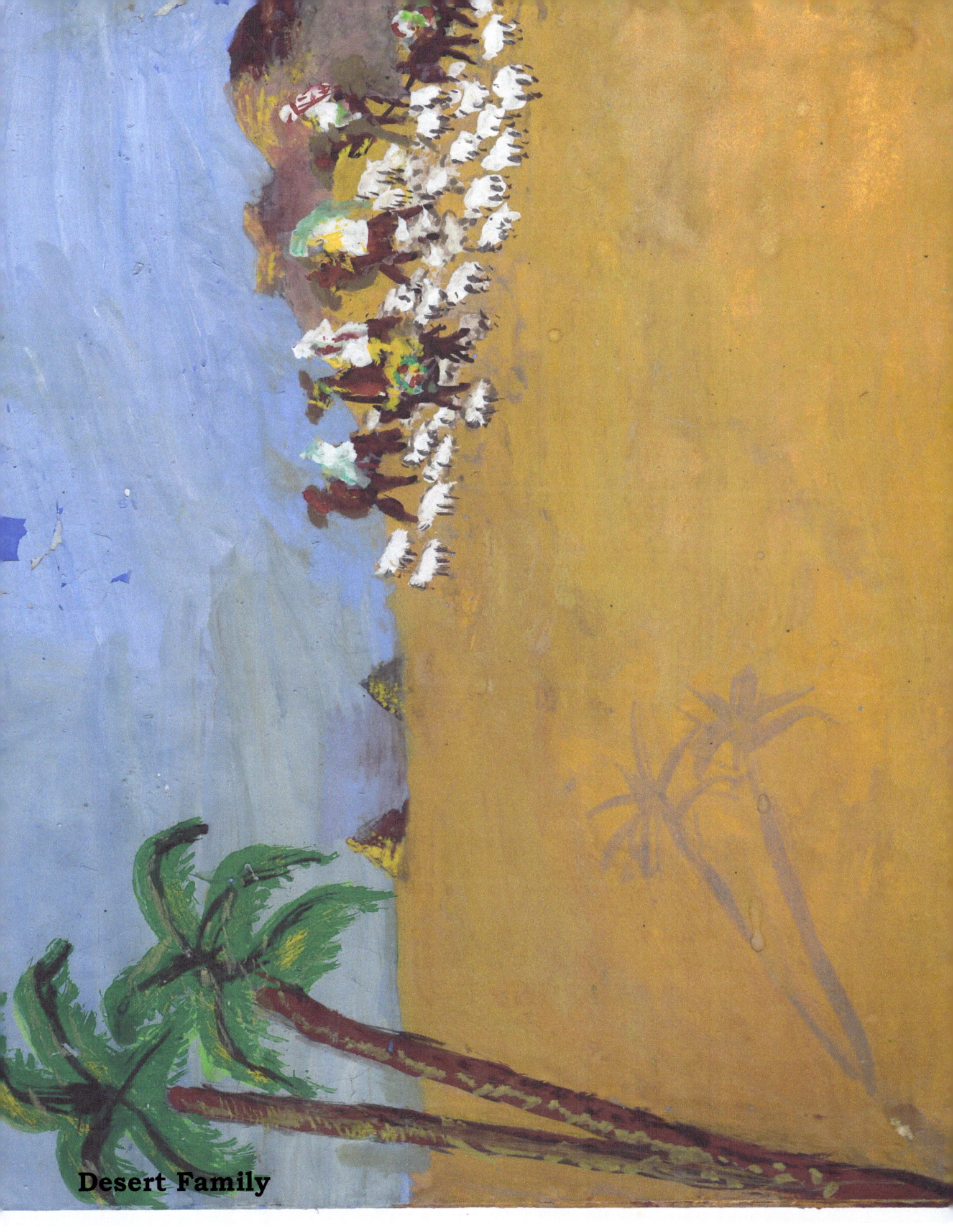

Desert Family

Horizon

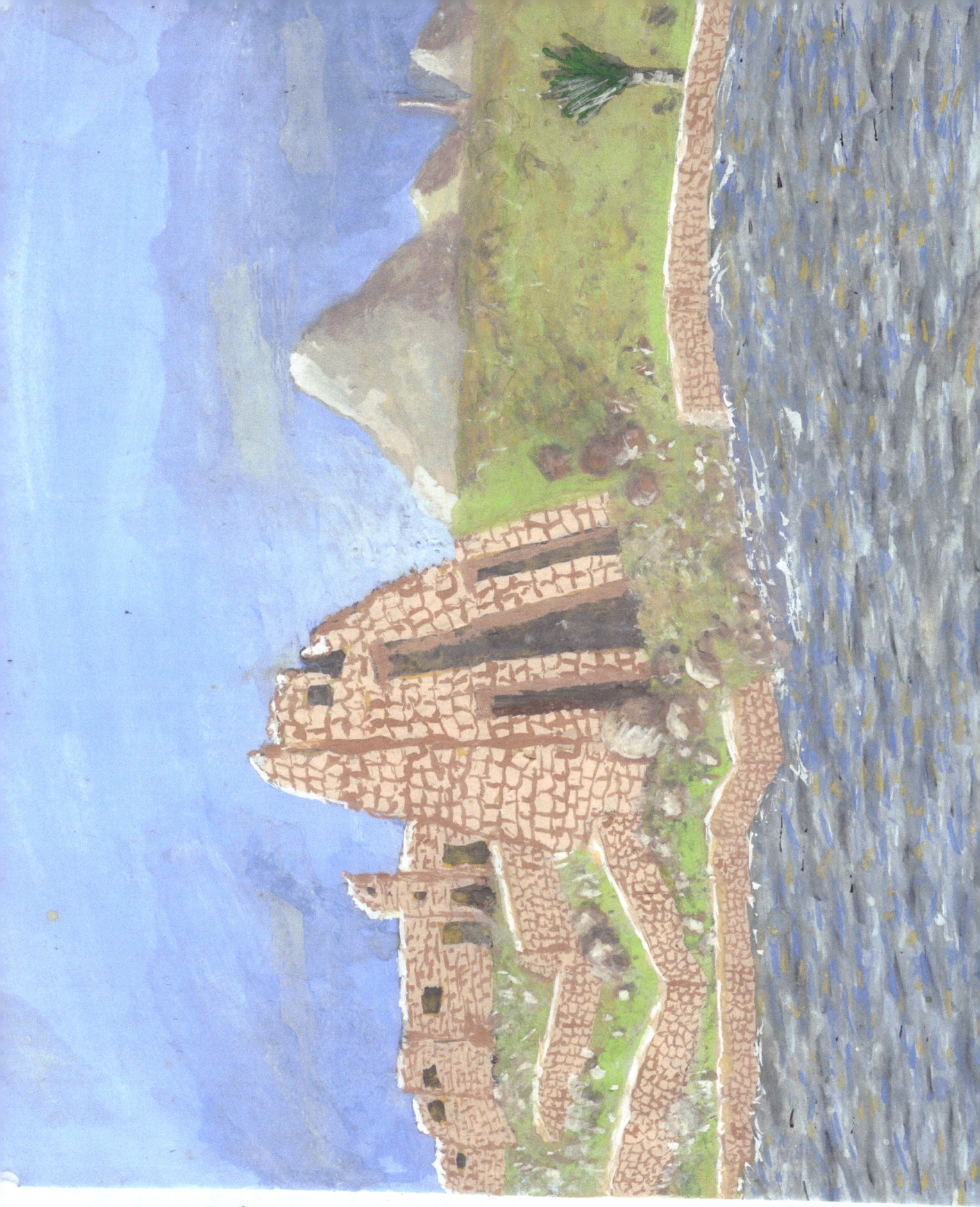

Ancient Culture

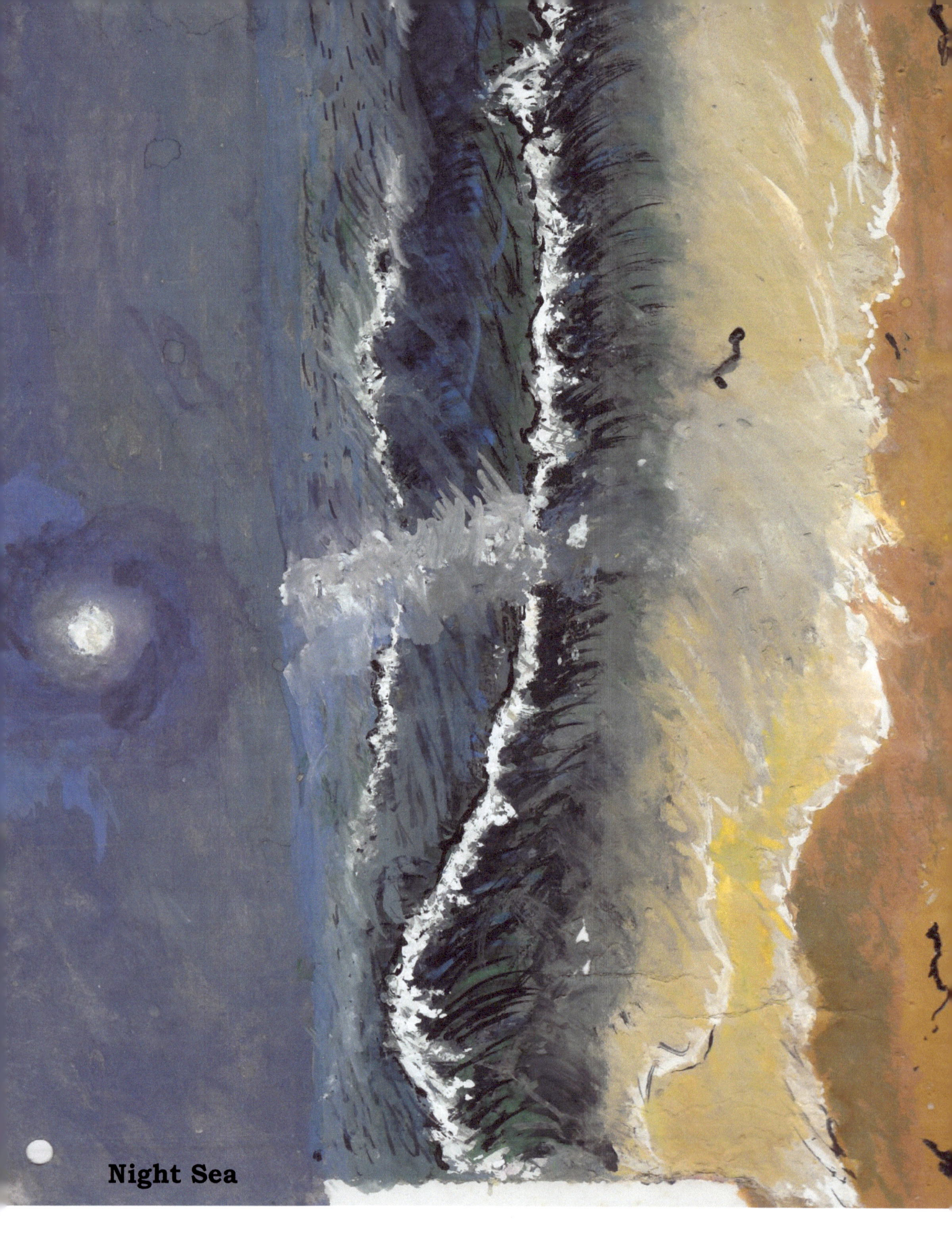

Night Sea

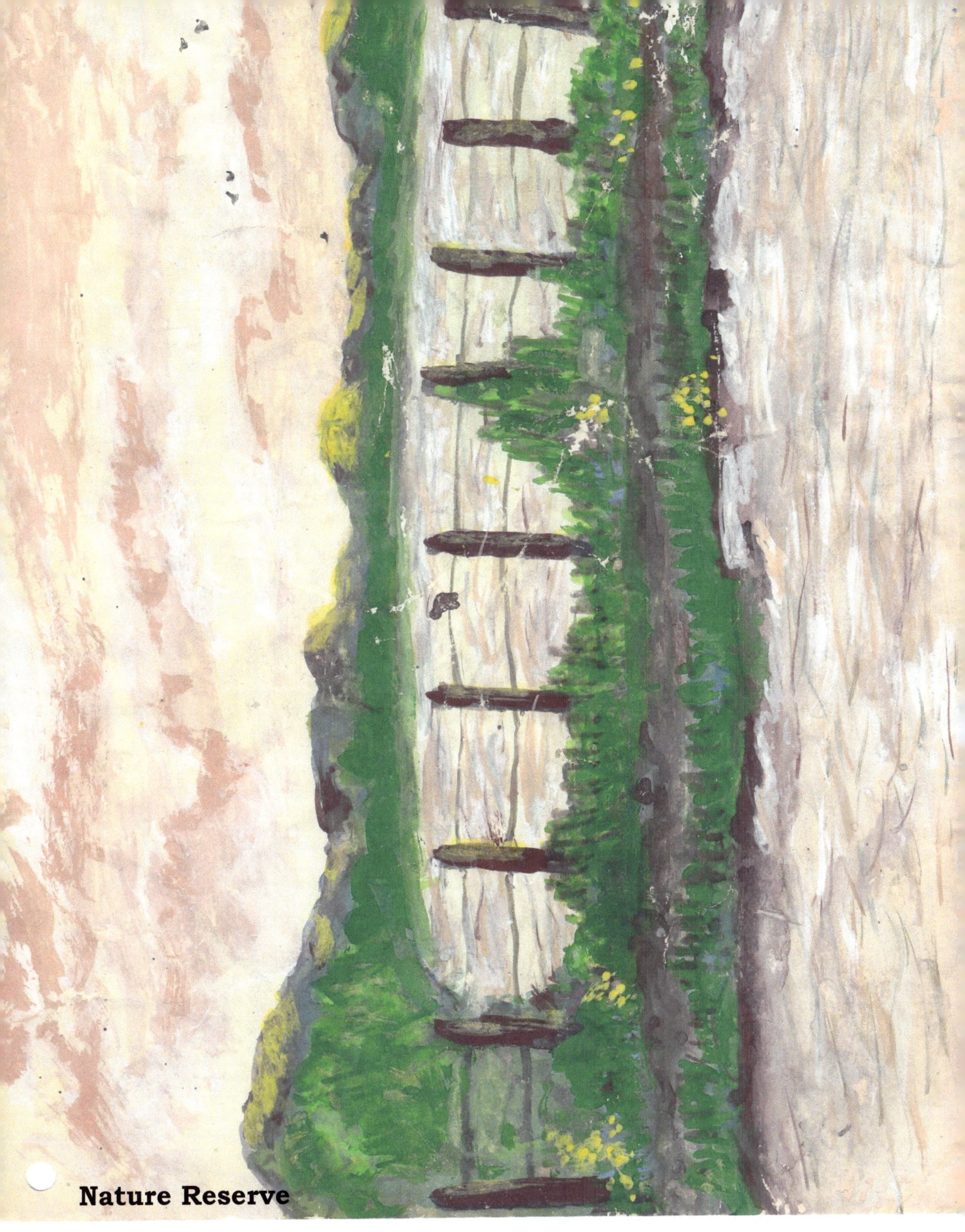

Nature Reserve

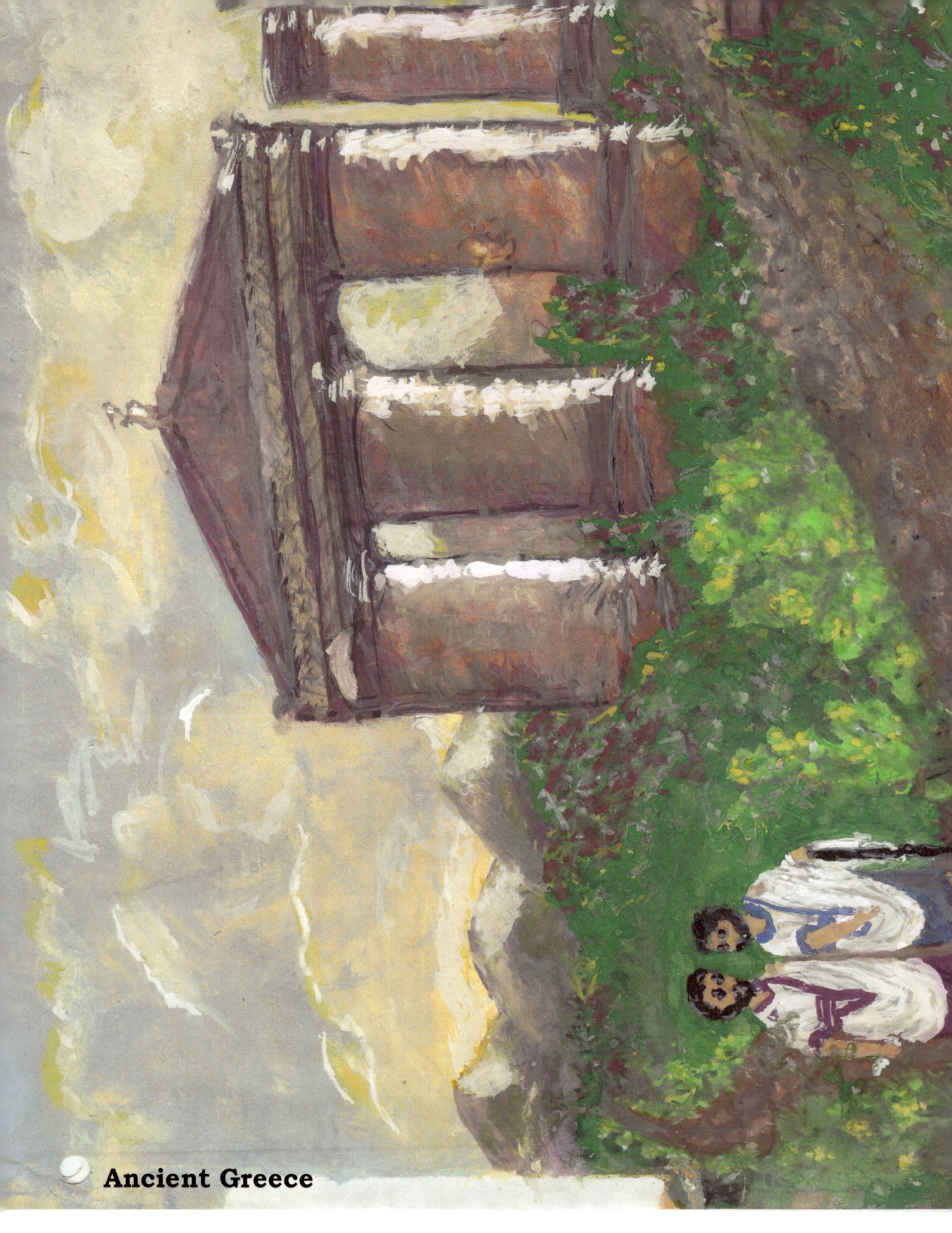

Ancient Greece